BFI Modern Classics

Rob White
Series Editor

Advancing into its second century, the cinema is now a mature art form with an established list of classics. But contemporary cinema is so subject to every shift in fashion regarding aesthetics, morals and ideas that judgments on the true worth of recent films are liable to be risky and controversial; yet they are essential if we want to know where the cinema is going and what it can achieve.

As part of the British Film Institute's commitment to the promotion and evaluation of contemporary cinema, and in conjunction with the influential BFI Film Classics series, BFI Modern Classics is a series of books devoted to individual films of recent years. Distinguished film critics, scholars and novelists explore the production and reception of their chosen films in the context of an argument about the film's quality and importance. Insightful, considered, often impassioned, these elegant, well-illustrated books will set the agenda for debates about what matters in modern cinema.

Blade Runner

Scott Bukatman

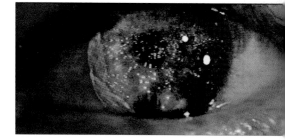

BFI PUBLISHING

This one is for Dana Polan:
scholar, friend, *mensch*

First published in 1997 by the
British Film Institute
21 Stephen Street, London W1P 2LN

The British Film Institute exists to promote
appreciation, enjoyment, protection and
development of moving image culture in and
throughout the whole of the United Kingdom.
Its activities include the National Film and
Television Archive; the National Film Theatre;
the Museum of the Moving Image;
the London Film Festival; the production and
distribution of film and video; funding and
support for regional activities; Library and
Information Services; Stills, Posters and
Designs; Research; Publishing and Education;
and the monthly *Sight and Sound* magazine.

Designed by Andrew Barron &
Collis Clements Associates.

Typeset in Garamond Simoncini
by Fakenham Photosetting Ltd.

Picture editing by Millie Simpson

Printed in Great Britain

British Library Cataloguing-in-Publication Data
A catalogue record for this book is available
from the British Library.
ISBN 0-85170-623-1

Contents

Acknowledgments 6

Introduction: On Seeing, Science
Fiction and Cities 7

1 Filming *Blade Runner* 13

2 The Metropolis 42

3 Replicants and Mental Life 64

Conclusion 86

Notes 87

Credits 91

Bibliography 94

Acknowledgments

Dana Polan suggested that I try to find 'another way' to approach a film that has been written about ad nauseam; these and other suggestions lodged themselves somewhere in my brain. My editor at the BFI, Rob White, was a careful and thoughtful reader, and his contribution is greater than he knows. Thanks to Edward Buscombe and Toby Miller for getting me involved with the BFI Modern Classics series. I stole some valuable ideas from Geoffrey Batchen and Stephanie Kessler. A course on Cinema and the City which I co-taught with Carla Yanni at the University of New Mexico in 1996 was a wonderful counterpoint to the preparation of this text, and I am indebted to those students who participated. In many ways, this project has its genesis in the 1994 Getty Center event, 'Cine City: Film and Perceptions of Urban Space 1895–1995'; Annette Michelson invited me to participate (I am *always* in *her* debt). Syd Mead and Douglas Trumbull were enthusiastic participants, and watching the film while sitting between the two of them was a remarkable treat (even if they *did* keep talking). Thanks to Erica Lynn Day for bibliographic assistance.

Picture credits

BFI Stills, Posters and Designs (cover). Moviestore (pp. 7, 38–9, 47, 51, 58, 67, 70, 78). Ronald Grant Archive (p. 79). Heavy Metal Communications, Inc. (p. 18). Syd Mead (pp. 32, 42). R.S.A. (p. 31). Blade Runner film stills and illustrations courtesy of Blade Runner Films/Warner Bros./R.S.A.

Introduction: On Seeing, Science Fiction and Cities

'I began to like New York, the racy, adventurous feel of it at night and the satisfaction that the constant flicker of men and women and machines gives to the restless eye.'

    F. Scott Fitzgerald, *The Great Gatsby*

'I want more life, *fucker* ...'

    Roy Batty, *Blade Runner*

'You Nexus, hah?' asks the wizened Asian technician at Eye Works. 'I designed your eyes.' Roy Batty, the android/replicant, briefly purses his lips in ironic amusement. 'Well, if only you could see what I've seen with

A spinner

your eyes.' Blade Runner is all about vision. Vision somehow both makes and unmakes the self in the film, creating a dynamic between a centred and autonomous subjectivity (eye/I) and the self as a manufactured, commodified object (Eye Works). The city is also known through vision. Vision actively makes the metropolitan world in a sustained encounter with delirious detail, yet because *Blade Runner* under-determines the lessons of that encounter, it effectively undermines interpretative certitudes. This science fiction adventure of urban perception produces an enhanced self-mastery, but also, at the same time, a dispossession, almost an erasure, of self.

Science fiction was always predicated upon continuous, perceptible change; it narrated a world that would become noticeably different over the course of a single lifetime. Those changes were part of the profound philosophical and political shifts of the 19th century, but they were most clearly connected to the rapid pace of technological development. The genre has been an essential part of technological culture for over a century. Through the language, iconography and narration of science fiction, the shock of the new is aestheticised and examined. Science fiction constructs a *space of accommodation* to an intensely technological existence, and this has continued through to the present electronic era.

It has also served as a vehicle for satire, social criticism and aesthetic estrangement. In its most radical aspect, science fiction narrates the dissolution of the most fundamental structures of human existence. By positing a world that behaves differently – whether physically or socially – from this one, our world is denaturalised. Science fiction even denaturalises language by emphasising processes of making meaning. The distance between the language of the text and the reader's lived experience represents the genre's ultimate subject. What science fiction offers, in Jameson's words, is 'the estrangement and renewal of our own reading present'.[1]

The brilliance of *Blade Runner*, like *Alien* before it, is located in its visual density. Scott's 'layering' effect produces an inexhaustible complexity, an infinity of surfaces to be encountered and explored, and unlike many contemporary films, *Blade Runner* refuses to explain itself. Even with the over-explicit narration of the original release, central issues were left un- or under-explained. Where are the 'off-world colonies'? Who goes there, and for what reason? Why does the city seem simultaneously crowded and empty? When and why were replicants created? When were they outlawed on Earth, and why? How does that 'Voight-Kampff test' work? The viewer of *Blade Runner* is forced to make constant inferences in order to understand the detailed world that the film presents.

This is how science fiction works, when it's working. Science fiction writer and literary theorist Samuel Delany argues that the distinctiveness of the genre comes from its unique demands on the reader. It demands inferential activity: sentences like 'The door dilated' (Robert Heinlein, *Starship Troopers*) or 'Daddy married, a man this time, and much more happily' (Thomas Disch, *334*) continually, and somewhat subtly, demonstrate the distance between the world of the reader and the world of the story, novel or film. Language alludes to the complexity of the world.[2]

Science fiction *film* also uses a complex 'language', but represents a special case because of its mainstream positioning and big-budget commodity status. Science fiction novels or comics need to sell only a few thousand copies to recoup their costs, so experimentalism is not discouraged, but the Hollywood blockbuster must find (or forge) a mass audience. Science fiction cinema's mode of production has committed it to proven, profitable structures, and so it is also more conservative. Yet although the narratives can be reactionary – and they often are – the delirious technological excesses of these films and their spectacular effects may 'speak' some other meaning entirely. The most significant 'meanings' of science fiction films are often found in their visual organisation and their emphasis on perception and 'perceptual selves'. Science fiction films continually thrust their spectators into new spaces that are alien and technologically determined. Cinematic movement becomes an essential mode of comprehension: the camera often takes on a subjective, first-person point of view when encountering such strange environments. Films as diverse as *2001*, *The Incredible Shrinking Man*, *Star Wars* and *Blade Runner* depend upon their dynamic visual complexity. In other words, they build worlds.

References to eyes abound in *Blade Runner* – not only are they a part of the *mise-en-scène* at Eye Works, but the film's third shot features a huge disembodied eye that stares unblinkingly at the infernal city spread before it, visible as an impossibly clear reflection. Replicants' eyes reflect a glowing red when the light hits them just right. Rick Deckard's replicant-detecting apparatus focuses on a subject's eye, magnifying it to read empathic responses. Memories, human or replicant, are linked to the recorded vision of photographs. The film was first set in the year 2020, but that was changed to 2019 because '2020' was associated with eye charts. Tyrell, the replicants' creator, wears glasses with bottle-thick lenses, and Roy gouges out his eyes. Pris's eyes open with an audible click, like Olympia's in *Tales of Hoffmann*. 'I've *seen* things you people wouldn't believe,' Roy declares at the point of dying. This, then, is a drama about vision.

But film is also a drama *of* vision, as Stephen Heath once noted,[3] and science fiction film is more centred on vision than most other genres. Viewscreens abound, along with telescopes, microscopes, scanning devices, X-ray vision and the scan-lined video-vision of robocops and terminators. Brooks Landon has written that the science fiction film produces its sense of wonder precisely from the presentation of new ways of seeing.[4] Unlike, say, horror or film noir, the genre privileges an aesthetics of presence: it *shows us stuff* . . .

Critics and audiences have continued to respond to the detailed vision of the future that *Blade Runner* offers. Ridley Scott has defined his characteristic method as *layering*: 'a kaleidoscopic accumulation of detail . . . in every corner of the frame'. A film, in his words, 'is a 700-layer cake'.[5] The film becomes a total environment that one inhabits in real time. Scott has compared film direction to orchestration, and 'every incident, every sound, every movement, every colour, every set, prop or actor' has significance within the 'performance' of the film.[6]

Blade Runner, with its sumptuously complex urban landscapes, demands to be actively watched; like Stanley Kubrick's *2001*, it emphatically returns its spectators to their own actions of perception and cognition.[7] Vision, especially in science fiction cinema, can be a tool of knowledge, but in *Blade Runner*, the more we see, the more our uncertainty grows. Its world features a profusion of simulations: synthetic animals, giant viewscreens, replicants, memory implants and faked photos are only some of them. Vision is no guarantee of truth, and the film's complexity encourages us to rethink our assumptions about perception by reminding us that, like memory, vision is more than a given, 'natural' process. There *is* no nature in *Blade Runner*.

The neurologist Oliver Sacks writes: 'When we open our eyes each morning, it is upon a world we have spent a lifetime learning to see. We are not given the world: we make our world through incessant experience, categorization, memory, reconnection.'[8] Science fiction film, along with more experimental forms of cinema, emphasises perception as activity: through these visual experiences, one realises that 'it is not a world that one perceives or constructs, but *one's own* world [that is] linked to a *perceptual self*, with a will, an orientation, and a style of its own'.[9] Replicants, forged memories and sumptuous surfaces make *Blade Runner* a film deeply concerned with the making and unmaking of selves, and with worlds that are no longer *given*.

Although it is generally regarded as exemplary of post-modernism, *Blade Runner* can be usefully read against 'The Metropolis and Mental Life', a 1903 essay by Georg Simmel, which drew a complicated portrait of the city as a site of emphatic sensation and kaleidoscopic variety. The 'swift and continuous shift of external and internal stimuli' provoked new mental attitudes in its inhabitants, and this 'intensification of emotional life' was neither entirely positive nor unswervingly negative.[10] A commitment to commerce reduced human beings to numbers or quantities, but the city's size also offered opportunities for exploration and growth, personal as well as economic. While 'the sphere of life of the small town is, in the main, enclosed within itself', the inner life of the metropolis 'extended in a wave-like motion over a broader national or international area'.[11] The economic imperatives of the city might 'hollow out the core of things' and flatten distinctions between people and objects, but it was an expansive environment: in the city, 'the individual's horizon is enlarged'.[12] It was easy to get lost in the metropolis; it was also possible to define oneself anew.

The same picture of the metropolis that Simmel drew in 1903 began to appear in the cinema at about the same time, and with a similar ambivalence. Cinema adroitly captured the city as a place of kaleidoscopic delirium and delight; a place of breakdown and rebirth. *Blade Runner*, with its probing camera and fine detail, revived this complex visual negotiation of urban space.

The anonymity that Simmel described as an unavoidable correlate of urban life extends in *Blade Runner* to an uncertainty about anyone's status as human or object. There could hardly be a better allegory for the quantifying and commodifying of human relations than the replicants – human as manufactured commodity, the *subject* as a literal *object* of exchange. But the film's intricate aesthetic and film noir-ish narrative also illustrated Simmel's proposition that 'The relationships and concerns of the typical metropolitan resident are so manifold and complex that … their relationships and activities intertwine with one another into a many-membered organism.'[13] *Blade Runner* is, in many ways, the quintessential city film: it presents urbanism as a lived heterogeneity, an ambiguous environment of fluid spaces and identities.

Like the best science fiction stories and city films, *Blade Runner* incorporates at once the magisterial gaze of the panorama, the sublime obscurity of the phantasmagoria and the shifting fields of the kaleidoscope. *Blade Runner*'s elaborate *mise-en-scène* and probing cameras create a tension that is fundamental to a period of inexorably advancing technological change. The inescapable and immersive city becomes a synecdoche for, and distillation of, all these unsettling technologies that continue to pervade lived experience. The film's aesthetic and its narrative underpinnings *magnify* and *enhance* the admixture of anxiety and delirium inherent to this experience. Its instability induces the epistemological and ontological uncertainties – the crises of knowing and being – that it narrates and theorises. Seeing is everything in *Blade Runner*, but it guarantees absolutely nothing.

1 Filming *Blade Runner*

Pre-production

The irony is that Philip K. Dick never got to see *Blade Runner*. Dick was one of the most prolific and brilliant of science fiction writers. His work is thoroughly paranoid and simultaneously witty and frightening, filled with slips of reality that are often only imperfectly repaired by story's end. In his earlier career, following unsuccessful attempts to succeed in the mainstream literary market, Dick began turning out pulpy science fiction tales in which different levels of reality continuously bumped up against each other, with a hapless protagonist struggling in the spaces between. A hallucinatory quality began to pervade the novels, and discussions of (and evocations of) psychosis and schizophrenic breakdown became increasingly prominent. Androids, mass media and religion all produced false realities, worlds of appearance that began to fall apart along with the minds of the protagonists. Drugs and psychosis, which both had their place in Dick's history, were frequently conduits to another reality, perhaps more real and perhaps not.

After decades of labour, Dick had achieved significant critical, if not financial, success in the United States – even more in France. His agent had sold the rights to his 1968 novel, *Do Androids Dream of Electric Sheep?* in 1974, but nothing was ever produced. As early as 1969, Jay Cocks and Martin Scorsese (who would collaborate in 1993 on *The Age of Innocence*) expressed interest, but the project got no further. In the mid-70s, Dick himself flirted with cinema, adapting his superb novel *UBIK* into a screenplay for Godard's sometime collaborator, Jean-Pierre Gorin. The screenplay was good too. Dick considered his new medium carefully: he wanted his film to end by regressing to flickering black and white silent footage, finally bubbling and burning to a halt. Once more, the project remained unproduced.

At about the same time, another writer began to wrestle with *Androids*, trying to fashion a screenplay from its diverse materials. Hampton Fancher was an actor and independent film-maker who aspired to produce for Hollywood. He was attracted by the novel's saturated air of paranoia and also, not incidentally, by its potential as an urban action film. The novel was optioned for Fancher by the actor Brian Kelly, and Kelly approached producer Michael Deeley, who was intrigued by the book, but not by its cinematic potential. Deeley suggested that a screenplay be prepared, and Fancher found himself, reluctantly, tagged as writer. The initial draft was completed in 1978, and Deeley began to shop it around.

Deeley had worked as an editor on *The Adventures of Robin Hood*, a television series produced in Britain, and first worked as a producer on *The Case of the Mukkinese Battlehorn* (1956), a stilted but occasionally inspired piece of Goonery with Spike Milligan and Peter Sellers. By the time Kelly and Fancher approached him, he'd gained some experience with science fiction, having produced *The Wicker Man* (1973) and *The Man Who Fell to Earth* (1976). Deeley had headed British Lion and Thorn-EMI, and also produced Peter Bogdanovich's *Nickelodeon* (1976) and Sam Peckinpah's *Convoy* (1978). His major critical success came with Michael Cimino's *The Deer Hunter*, which received the Academy Award for Best Picture in 1978.

Deeley approached Ridley Scott, a former set-designer for the BBC who had directed episodes of *Z-Cars* and other programmes for British television before producing hundreds of commercials, many strikingly stylish. His first feature was *The Duellists* (1977), an adaptation of a Joseph Conrad story, and a very effective blend of naturalistic and stylised elements. His next work, *Alien*, was in post-production: it would turn out to be a charged telling of a familiar story. Already Scott's hallmark was a visual density that revealed as much as, or more than, the script. The characters inhabited complex worlds that provided oblique contexts for their decisions and actions. There could be, in Scott's best work, no psychology without an accompanying sociology, no individual in isolation.

At first, however, Scott declined the project. He was committed to a number of large-scale assignments, including *Dune* for Dino de

Laurentiis (David Lynch finally directed *Dune* which, despite its strengths, is a case-study in how *not* to adapt a popular science fiction novel), and was understandably resistant to being typecast as a science fiction director. But personal difficulties led him back to *Blade Runner*, a project that he hoped to begin immediately, although it would be fully a year before shooting could commence. Scott joined the production in late February 1980.

As all this was going on, *Star Wars* was released. Before its appearance, science fiction was not a commercially viable Hollywood genre. The lively matinees of the 50s were the stuff of the past, and science fiction cinema in the 60s and 70s had provided a mix of modernist obscurity (*Alphaville*, *2001*, *Solaris*, *The Man Who Fell to Earth*) and Saturday-afternoon dystopianism (*Soylent Green*, *Logan's*

Dystopia by firelight

Run, Westworld). The expansionism that once almost defined the genre had yielded to collapse, implosion and the overwhelming sense of a future of exhausted possibility.

Star Wars opened in May 1977 and quickly became one of the most popular films in Hollywood history. While its initial success was predicted by no one, the history of this saga exemplified the strategies of the post-classical Hollywood film industry. In 1975, *Jaws* had remade the marketing wisdom of Hollywood by finding and exploiting a summer audience with uncanny dexterity. *Star Wars* reaped the benefits of this new cinematic season. Its combination of old-fashioned romantic swashbuckling and new computer-driven camera effects proved irresistible to older and younger audiences alike, while its innate gentleness was acceptable to mainstream audiences of both genders. George Lucas had produced a futuristic film steeped in not-so-subtle nostalgia – for Hollywood adventure, for science fiction's expansiveness, and for a future reassuringly set 'a long time ago in a galaxy far, far away'. The film's success, along with that of Steven Spielberg's gargantuan, sentimental *Close Encounters of the Third Kind*, established the centrality of science fiction as a Hollywood genre. Technically innovative but ultimately (very) reassuring and familiar, these were canny blends. (The combination of narrative conservatism and technical wizardry had predecessors at other points in Hollywood history, most evidently at the Disney studio in the late'30s and early 40s.) Budgets for science fiction films were increased accordingly.

Blade Runner was to be produced through a small company, Filmways Pictures, at a fairly limited budget of $13 million. But before principal photography could begin, the script needed to be reworked. Repeatedly. Fancher ultimately produced eight separate drafts, closely supervised by the director. Scott told him to begin thinking about what lay outside the windows; about what constituted *the world* of the film. When Fancher admitted that he hadn't yet considered these elements, Scott told him to look at *Metal Hurlant*, a rather lavishly produced French comics magazine (published in English as *Heavy Metal*) that had attracted some of the form's most innovative creators. *Heavy Metal* artists produced visually dense science fiction fantasies with baroque designs, airbrushed colour and elaborate linework, as well as highly exaggerated scenes of violence and sex. The aesthetic of *Blade Runner* derives heavily from a number of these creators: Moebius's compacted urbanism, Philippe Druillet's saturated darkness and Angus McKie's scalar exaggerations come easily to mind.

Disagreements between Fancher and Scott were multiplying, however. While Scott continued to elaborate on the atmospheric world outside the windows, he was also winnowing down the complexity of the story, and Fancher was resisting. With the start of shooting only two months away another writer, David Peoples, was hired to complete the script. Peoples was an editor and aspiring screenwriter: he had edited the Oscar-winning 1977 documentary *Who Are the Debolts? (And Where Did They Get 19 Kids?)*, co-written and co-edited *The Day After Trinity* in 1980, and would later script Clint Eastwood's *Unforgiven* (1992). Peoples said that 'Ridley was sort of heading toward the spirit of *Chinatown*. Something more mysterious and foreboding and threatening.'[14] The actual shooting script was an amalgam of Fancher's work, Peoples's December 1980 rewrite and a later partial rewrite by Fancher. Peoples has been credited with tightening the mystery aspects of the screenplay and deepening the humanity of the android adversaries, now known as *replicants*.

Scott, revealing an awareness of the textures of science fiction, had been toying with the role of language in his strange new world. He wanted to find new names for the protagonist's profession as well as his targets – *detective*, *bounty hunter* and *androids* were overly familiar terms, no longer evocative enough. Fancher, rummaging through his library, found William Burroughs's *Blade Runner: A Movie*, which was a reworking of an Alan E. Nourse novel about smugglers of medical supplies ('blade runner' also sounds a *lot* like 'bounty hunter', Deckard's profession in the novel). The rights to the title were purchased from Burroughs and Nourse. 'Replicant' was the contribution of Peoples, whose microbiologist daughter suggested some variation on 'replication'. The substitution of unexplained terms such as blade runner and replicant for more familiar ones was typical of Scott's approach, which was rooted in an intriguing combination of the specific and the suggestive.

As the script was being finalised in December 1980, Filmways balked at the expense and withdrew from the project. Over the next two weeks, Michael Deeley managed to put together a new financing arrangement. There would be three participants, providing an initial total budget of $21.5 million (later raised to $28 million – up considerably from the original $13 million estimate). The Ladd Company put up $7.5 million through Warner Bros., which was granted the domestic distribution rights for the film; Sir Run Run Shaw put up

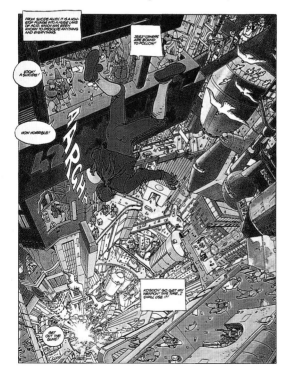

The headlong imaginings of Moebius in *Heavy Metal*

the same amount in exchange for the foreign rights; and Tandem Productions, a company run by Norman Lear, Bud Yorkin and Jerry Perechino, put up the remaining $7 million for the ancillary rights (television, video, etc.). Tandem also served as completion bond guarantors for *Blade Runner*, which gave them the right to take over the picture if it went over budget by 10 per cent.[15]

The Look of the Future

Alien must have been tremendously valuable preparation for *Blade Runner*. While its story was filled with horror film clichés that existed uncomfortably within the high-technology spaceship settings, the design of the film raised it to another level of importance. Scott divided the design responsibilities, so that H.R. Giger, for example, was only responsible for the design of the alien beings and artifacts. Meanwhile, the spaceship-tugboat *Nostromo*, with a vast ore-processing factory in tow, was a masterpiece of corridors and cluttered lived-in spaces, and Scott's hand-held cameras and use of available light gave the film an almost documentary-like authority. The design and casting of *Alien* raised issues pertaining to race, class and gender, most of which were only briefly suggested by the film's script. The environment of the film became its most potent site of meaning, even before the appearance of Giger's stunningly complex alien creature. Alongside the film's unlikely narrative events, Scott succeeded in creating a masterfully plausible and nuanced space.

The spaceship as factory, drifting in the voids of interstellar space, recalls the *Pequod* of *Moby Dick*, which in Melville's hands became a foundry, an infernal intrusion of culture into the natural environment.[16] The comparison is further justified by the aesthetic of *Blade Runner*, with its city that resembles nothing so much as a vast, boundless refinery, and its world that no longer contains any trace of nature.

Ridley Scott has said that *Blade Runner* 'is a film set forty years hence, made in the style of forty years ago',[17] and this combination informs everything from the narrative to the design and photography.

The story borrows liberally from the private-eye genre, via the films noir of the 40s and 50s. The voice-over narration (which was, in fact, always part of the conception but was less pervasive), the alienated hero with a questionable moral compass, the *femme fatale*, the Los Angeles setting, the movement from high-class penthouses to lower-class dives: all of these are familiar – indeed, overfamiliar – trappings of noir. Dick was openly upset with Fancher's drafts, and had good reason to complain of 'the old cliché-ridden Chandleresque figure' at the centre of the narrative (he called early versions 'Philip Marlowe meets the Stepford Wives').

Scott's own artistic sensibilities were hugely important in the development of the project: he was capable of dashing off useful sketches that could guide writers, designers or storyboard artists. Michael Deeley and production designer Lawrence Paull, among others, have given Scott much of the credit for *Blade Runner*'s design. His future city was informed by a range of sources: engravings by Hogarth and paintings by Vermeer, photographs by Jacob Riis of New York's Lower East Side, the urban nightdreams of Edward Hopper and the baroque visual science fiction of *Heavy Metal*. What was needed was some means of unifying these disparate visions, of shaping a future that was close enough to touch.

Syd Mead, a commercial and industrial designer as well as an ardent science fiction reader, was hired as *Blade Runner*'s 'visual futurist'. Mead had been imagining things for decades, first for various American corporations, including Ford, US Steel and Sony, then as a freelance designer and illustrator. In his career he has designed automobiles, yachts, nightclubs and the interiors of privately owned jumbo jets. His first film work was designing the massive V'ger construct for 1979's *Star Trek: The Motion Picture* (his model was photographed by Douglas Trumbull's EEG unit). *Blade Runner*, however, offered something different: the opportunity to extrapolate a detailed future world that remained deeply rooted in lived, physical experience. 'The essence of my work', Mead has written, 'is an involvement with the total scenario; the world of an idea made into an article and the translation of fantasy into visual fact.'[18] Small wonder that the industrial designer of 'total scenarios' should become involved with the film director of 'total environments'.

Mead was only hired to produce designs for *Blade Runner*'s vehicles, and he tried to base these on his understanding of technology, socio-economic conditions and the personalities of the characters. His rich sketches with their futuristic settings, however, persuaded Scott to put Mead in charge of street scenes and interiors as well. Scott admired how Mead's speculations remained grounded in plausible engineering principles; he provided the film with a disciplined, unifying visual imagination.[19]

The dominant strategy in designing *Blade Runner*'s future was 'retrofitting', which, according to Mead, 'simply means upgrading old machinery or structures by slapping new add-ons to them'.[20] The future, in other words, is a combination of the new and the very, very used, just like the present: the utopian fantasies of *Things to Come* (1936), with its gleaming new Everytown, are no longer economically, ecologically or politically supportable, even in dreams and fictions.

The major set for the film, nicknamed 'Ridleyville' during the production, was the New York Street at Burbank Studios; built in 1929, it had been the setting for numerous Warner Bros. crime films and noirs. Mead studied photographs of the site, and began adding on patches, ducts, rewirings, expansions, lights and grime. Retrofitted detailing was laid over the backlot façades (Paul Sammon points out that the new setting was thus 'retrofitted' over an older one). The New York Street set was loaded with neon and the streets were filled with what the publicity notes called 'a variety of mechanical stuff'. The 'stuff' was remarkable, even obsessive, but crucial: newsstands featured the latest issues (one assumes) of *Krotch*, *Kill* and *MONI* magazines; parking meters warned of lethal consequences for vandals; and video monitors, called 'trafficators', provided traffic information and directional signals.

Elaborate matte-paintings were also important to *Blade Runner*'s

(Overleaf) Bright lights, big city

look by allowing further layers of retrofitting, such as the huge towers that loom above the city's street scenes. They are especially evident outside Deckard's apartment and in the rooftop battle between Deckard and Batty. Mead's original designs served as guides for the finished paintings by Matthew Yuricich. Yuricich had been working on effects for decades, and his credits included the brilliant matte-work on *Forbidden Planet* (1956). The scene with Pris walking along a street was originally designed to include a high-angle shot revealing a multi-layered freeway system below her (as in urban science fiction comics by Moebius). Yuricich had done something similar in *Forbidden Planet*, including the use of a beam of light to focus attention on the diminutive, walking figure(s).[21]

The mixture of periods defines the film's set design: futuristic hovercars, called 'spinners', travel through the city, while some retrofitted Plymouths and Cadillacs continue to cruise the streets. Costumes and hairstyles were also borrowed from earlier styles, helping to avoid the science fiction cliché of overly uniform clothing or hair. Rachael is the most evidently '40s', resembling an upscale Mildred Pierce when we first see her (Pauline Kael remarked that her shoulder entered the scene long before she did). Pris and Roy quote punk hairstyles, which Roy supplements with clothing of militaristic greys and blacks.

Special Effects

Special effects are an important part of cinema's experiential dimension: they can bring the visual, auditory and even tactile and kinaesthetic conditions of perception to the foreground of the viewer's consciousness. *Blade Runner*'s sumptuous effects were produced by EEG (Entertainment Effects Group), a partnership between Douglas Trumbull and Richard Yuricich (Matthew's younger brother). The two had worked with *Blade Runner*'s associate producer Ivor Powell on *2001*.

Trumbull's work is especially interesting: he created the psychedelic Stargate effects for *2001* and the lovely lightships of *Close*

Encounters of the Third Kind. He also directed two features, *Silent Running* (1971) and *Brainstorm* (1983) while developing his 65mm, 60fps Showscan exhibition system. A Trumbull sequence is less the description of an *object* than the construction of an *environment*; this is especially apparent in *Blade Runner*'s gorgeous and monstrous Los Angeles. He has expressed dissatisfaction with the flatness of earlier effects work, which required cutaways to distract the audience: 'I like the idea of creating some crazy illusion that looks so great that you can really hang on it like a big master shot of an epic landscape.'[20] Trumbull's effects are profound and contemplative, and in each film that features his work there is at least one sequence where the characters stare mutely at the marvels they behold. These spectacular fields – the Stargate, the Mothership, Los Angeles 2019 – testify to the sublimity of technology, an experience of its beauty infused with the anxiety that acknowledges its power. Trumbull's sequences are different from most other effects work in that they reveal an ambivalence towards technology. They are neither celebratory nor condemning, but instead articulate a tension between uneasiness and identification as viewers try to assimilate the artificial infinities of his technological environments. These effects also testify to the beauty and terrifying power of the cinema, which is itself a technological marvel of vision.

After the disappointments of the *Brainstorm* production, Trumbull gave up on Hollywood, which was, he said, 'multiplexing itself to death', and began developing multimedia forms for theme parks and World's Fairs. An attention to spectacle and exhibition connects Trumbull's work to early cinema and pre-cinematic entertainment. Just as eighteenth- and nineteenth-century panoramas and dioramas once incorporated motion, lighting and sound effects, Trumbull has developed the 'Ridefilm Theatre', a simulator-theatre system with a fifteen-passenger motion base encompassed by a 180 degree spherically curved screen. High-resolution images are projected with synchronised movement to produce a strong sense of kinetic involvement in a complex technological space. The popularity of these simulation rides has provided him with new opportunities to experiment with experiential cinema. He is currently a vice-president of the IMAX Corporation, which has been experimenting with large format, 3-D film presentation. His work continues to be characterised by a strong sense of *presence*, enhanced by extensive subjective camera movement and visual immersion, whether in Cinerama or Showscan or simulators.

The effects budget for *Blade Runner* was originally $2 million for thirty-eight shots, later expanded to $3.5 million for a total of ninety separate shots. This was still a limited budget, and several scenes, notably an opening sequence of Deckard entering the city on a high-speed train, had to be jettisoned in the planning stage. Effects production for *Blade Runner* extended from March to December of 1981.[23] Trumbull was involved only until about one-third of the way through principal photography, when his *Brainstorm* project (a film about a fantasied 'total cinema' that could record and play back sensory experience, emotions and memories) was finally given the go-ahead by MGM. After Trumbull's departure, David Dryer took control of the special effects unit, with evident success (Trumbull continued to participate in a more supervisory capacity), but the finished film still bears Trumbull's stylistic stamp. In addition, Trumbull's characteristic production methods were used: the effects were first produced on 65mm stock for enhanced resolution, and then the footage was reduced to an anamorphic 35mm negative. Any live action scenes that would require the later addition of special effects were also shot in 65mm, in order to avoid the increased graininess that marked most pre-digital effects work. The integration of live action with effects had rarely been so effectively planned or executed.

Trumbull has enjoyed claiming that he was bored by the *Blade Runner* production because it required few technical innovations. But there were some challenges. The near-future setting put an increased emphasis on plausibility; atmospheric effects had to be carefully planned to provide the sense of smog, fog and gigantic scale upon which the look of the film would largely depend. Trumbull had designed a 'smoke room' (actually, vaporised low-grade diesel fuel), which was used extensively on *Blade Runner* to blur details and produce a sense of aerial perspective and distance. Smoke served multiple purposes in the film, enhancing the romantic, noir look of the city while summoning a general unhealthy haze and convincing perspective to the miniatures.

The Tyrell pyramids were constructed on an elaborate 8-foot deep model which included thousands of windows that could be illuminated from behind. The panoramic Los Angeles of the opening sequence was popularly known as the Hades set, for reasons that should be obvious. It was a miniature set, 18 feet long and 13 feet deep. The foreground buildings were three-dimensional miniatures, giving way to two-dimensional models nearer the background. The Hades set was constructed on a raised platform to permit lighting from below, and

The Tyrell Corporation

featured forced perspectives to exaggerate the sense of depth and compensate for optical distortions caused by the camera lens.

To photograph the Hades set, Trumbull used his computer-controlled camera – the first – originally developed for *Close Encounters*.[24] Such 'motion-control' cameras made it possible to reproduce camera movements with absolute precision by computing the changing relations between visual elements. Multiple 'passes' over and around each object and background element would supply separate pieces of film that could be composed into a seamlessly matched whole. In addition, the camera itself could become an active, gliding agent, fully interacting with the world onscreen.[25]

Much attention was paid to the spinners, the flying cars. Mead designed them with masses of jutting elements for the retrofitted look, many of which suggested their functions. They featured 'twist-wrist' hydraulic steering, gull-winged doors that opened vertically and internal lifting turbines. The interior sported an impressive set of read-outs, including one for an onboard computer and a sensor for reading traffic patterns. Miniatures were constructed on a variety of scales, depending upon the requirements of the shot: an 18-inch model was used for more distant camera setups, since it was more manoeuvrable than the 4-foot version. A full-sized model was used for the street scenes.[26]

An interesting technique was used for objects flying in depth, such as the spinners' flight over Los Angeles in the first sequence. As the object receded into the distance, the exposure on it would be reduced and the matte photographed less clearly. As a result, the object became 'contaminated' by the background images; in other words, background and object would blur together slightly, as though the object was disappearing into a real distance instead of simply shrinking on the screen.

Cinematography

It is difficult to imagine *Blade Runner* without the exceptional cinematography of Jordan Cronenweth, who had previously worked with

Robert Altman (*Brewster McCloud*, 1970), Jonathan Demme (*Handle with Care*, 1977; *Stop Making Sense*, 1984) and Ken Russell (*Altered States*, 1980); he would subsequently direct photography for Francis Ford Coppola (*Peggy Sue Got Married*, 1986; *Gardens of Stone*, 1987). The film's noir conception needed to evoke romanticism and urban chaos, and the photography had to create a pervasive claustrophobia that would not overwhelm the audience.[27] It also had to blend with the effects footage that Trumbull and Dryer were supervising.

Cronenweth's characteristic method, especially on interiors, involved combining a soft frontlight (sometimes a soft uplight), with a hard backlight, creating intense silhouettes and haloes; the addition of smoke or reflective effects in the background further abstracted the space. The end results were crisp, even harsh, while remaining hazy and glamorous. The street scenes, on the other hand, were often shot with a hand-held camera, using the available light from Ridleyville's dozens of neon signs (some of the neon had been used in Coppola's *One from the Heart*, released in 1982). If more light was needed, more neon would be added to the set.[28] These scenes are more jittery, and certainly more harsh. The street, after all, is where the replicant Zhora is killed, smashing through layers of plate-glass windows and crashing to the floor amid piles of anonymous mannequins.

Blade Runner's city rejects boundaries between public and private. Beams of light strafe the innermost recesses of apartments and alleys. Cronenweth said that the lights were used 'for both advertising and crime control, much the way a prison is monitored by moving search lights. The shafts of light represent invasion of privacy by a supervising force, a form of control. You are never sure who it is . . .'.[29] Replicants are programmed with false memories, a further dissolution of personal space: even the private territories of the mind become vulnerable to attack.

Tensions and Post-production
Principal photography began on 9 March 1981, and was completed a long four months later, on 9 July. By all accounts, it was a nightmarish

production. Hollywood was not entirely prepared for this British director's autocratic style, and Scott was equally unprepared for the facts of life in unionised Hollywood. It should be understood, however, that a production of *Blade Runner*'s conceptual complexity required managing an overwhelming accumulation of details in the set construction, props, costuming and lighting, and further, that footage from the live shoot would need to be perfectly synchronised with the film produced by the effects team. Nevertheless, as the shoot proceeded, it became apparent that director and crew were not getting along, and neither was the director with his star, Harrison Ford, or Ford with Sean Young.

Meanwhile, the relationship with Tandem, which held a completion bond on the film, was uncomfortable almost from the start. Yorkin and Perechino (Lear was not involved with *Blade Runner*) had

Artificial eyes

little confidence in the vision of the film's creators, especially as the production fell increasingly behind schedule. Scott insisted on immediately reshooting the entire first two weeks of material, after deciding that the original footage was simply too dark. It's also very possible that Tandem was beginning to realise that they had not funded an action-adventure of the order of *Star Wars*.[30] The financial backers were increasingly upset about Scott's on-set perfectionism, which revealed itself in seemingly endless retakes (Sammon writes that fifteen to twenty takes were the norm). By the end of shooting, the film was already $5 million over budget. On 11 July, according to the terms of their original agreement, Tandem stepped in to take over the production.

The organisation's first action was, essentially, to fire Scott and Deeley, although this was more along the lines of a technical notification than an actuality. Tandem did, however, begin to exercise significant and increasing control over the production. The screenings for the financiers were apparently depressed and depressing affairs: 'This movie gets worse every screening,' was one Tandem comment. In the eyes of the Tandem producers *Blade Runner* was morose and narratively muddled, but they were hardly interested in the expensive reshooting ideas that Scott and Deeley proposed.

Preliminary
owl-sketches

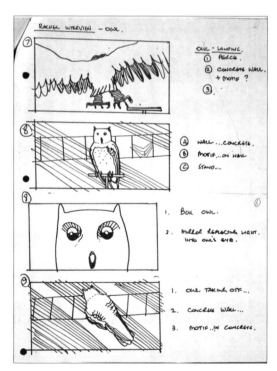

Disastrous sneak previews in Dallas and Denver were held in early March 1982. The negative comments concentrated on narrative confusion, the film's slow pace and the unresolved ending, in which Deckard and Rachael board the elevator to escape the law. To resolve these problems, Tandem insisted on a number of changes, two of which effectively reshaped the entire experience of *Blade Runner*.

First, there was the addition of explanatory narration, an idea that had been part of Fancher's earlier drafts, but was only minimally present in the filmed version. While the shooting script had largely jettisoned the voice-overs, it was always assumed that they might be restored later if needed. Three versions were recorded: the first was written by Daryl Ponicsan, and was considered ineffective. Peoples then constructed an amalgam of Fancher's and his own lines. After the screenings for

Pre-production artwork by Syd Mead

Tandem, Scott eliminated nearly all of the narration, except for Deckard's response to Batty's death. However, following the sneak previews, Bud Yorkin supervised a third attempt, this one written largely by television writer Roland Kibbee and recorded without Scott's or Deeley's participation. Persistent rumours have circulated that Harrison Ford, who had never liked the idea of the narration anyway, tried to sabotage this final recording with an impossibly flat delivery.

Tandem's other major contribution to the reshaping of *Blade Runner* was the happy ending, in which Deckard and Rachael soar over surprisingly pristine landscapes (comprised of out-takes from Kubrick's opening montage for *The Shining*) as Deckard informs us that Rachael, mysteriously, had no termination date. Again, as other writers have emphasised, this ending was anticipated by earlier versions of the script, but Scott's increasing insistence on ambiguity (as well as very real time and budget difficulties) led him to prefer an ending in which Gaff's line, 'It's too bad she won't live! But then again, who does?' would resonate with the audience as the credits rolled.

Responding to the Replicants

Blade Runner opened on 25 June 1982 throughout the United States. The initial response to the film could not have been entirely unexpected, but it was still grievously disappointing. Neither critics nor the public were prepared for the pensive darkness of the finished work. In the *New Yorker*, Pauline Kael admitted that 'a visionary sci-fi movie that has its own look can't be ignored', but, she added, 'If anybody comes around with a test to detect humanoids, maybe Ridley Scott and his associates should hide.'[31] Kael was not only sharper about the story's shortcomings than any other critic (then or now), she also criticised the lack of sustained erotic tension with which a Sternberg or Nicolas Roeg would have invested the film's dissipated decadence.

Janet Maslin of the *New York Times* found the film 'muddled yet mesmerizing', while Gene Siskel wrote in the *Chicago Tribune* that the film 'looks terrific but is empty at its core'.[32] Reviews in *Time, Newsweek* and *The New Republic* praised the complexity of the film's aesthetics but maintained reservations about the narrative. Most critics missed an overtly humanist side to the film – a clear indication as to what being human *was* and what it *meant*. *Blade Runner* was not a film designed to provide straightforward answers to those questions. Its dehumanised world – the world that Scott and the production crew had laboured over – superficially blocked the very possibility of humanist survival, yet subtle signs of its existence echoed through the cacophony of the city.

Science fiction fans were not immediately any more perceptive, although they ultimately formed the core of the film's emergent cult audience. *Blade Runner* shared nothing (other than the casting of Harrison Ford) with the affirmative, hugely kinetic adventures of Luke Skywalker and Indiana Jones and the USS *Enterprise*. These works dichotomised good and evil and sent them into pitched battle. *Blade Runner*'s world was neither so certain nor so resolved: it offered a framework for doubt. On the other hand, for those viewers who had been awaiting another *2001* or *Alphaville*, *Blade Runner* made immediate sense as a serious attempt to explore the intricate surfaces of urban culture and exploit the visuality of science fiction.

The film's opening weekend receipts totalled $6.15 million – not much for a wide release on 1,290 screens – and they dropped steadily from there.[33] The final earnings on the film's initial theatrical run were only about $14 million – or half of its production budget. Circumstances, however, were fortuitous for keeping *Blade Runner* before the public, and its audience continued to grow. As Paul Sammon has pointed out, 'One of the sudden (and major) catalysts behind *Blade Runner*'s resurgence was the sudden, near-simultaneous expansion of the cable television and home video markets.'[34] Faced with the disappointing box office, Warners pulled the film from distribution earlier than usual in order to broadcast it on its own Warner-Amex Satellite Entertainment Network. The film's release on video also did well, not unusual in itself for a big-budget science fiction film, but it became one of the most rented tapes on the market. The usual science

(Opposite) Sepia fashion

fiction cult discovered it, but the film's density and complexity encouraged repeat viewings even among lay audiences. Another sign of the film's emerging success came when Criterion released a high-priced laser-disk version with the widescreen ratio preserved and some supplemental materials: it was their top-selling disk for several years.

The audience continued to grow. In 1982, *Cityspeak*, the first fanzine dedicated to the film, appeared. The next year, *Blade Runner* was voted the Third Most Favourite Science Fiction Film of All Time (following *Star Wars* and *2001*) at the World Science Fiction Convention. An anthology of scholarly writings on the film appeared in 1991, which included essays on the architecture, gender issues, genre issues and problems of textual adaptation. The film was also rapidly becoming a touchstone for writers on post-modern culture, and provocative work on the film was produced by such prominent cultural theorists as Guiliana Bruno, Andrew Ross, Kaja Silverman, Vivian Sobchack and Slavoj Žižek.[35]

Blade Runner Revised and Revisited: The Director's Cut

Interest in the film was significantly boosted when Michael Arick, a film sound preservationist, found what he first thought was a rare 70mm print in the Todd-AO vaults. After a few months of effort he secured the print for the Warners archives, where it remained until a May 1990 screening at the Los Angeles Cineplex Odeon Fairfax Theatre, which was mounting a retrospective of 70mm prints. The Sunday morning screening was sold out, already attesting to growing popular interest, but the film shown that day was not the *Blade Runner* with which the world had become familiar. From the text of the opening crawling titles to the virtual absence of narration, to the way the story ended, significant differences existed throughout.

The print was screened for Ridley Scott, who recognised it as a workprint used for the Denver and Dallas sneak previews. The sound mix was crude and the Vangelis score was absent from the final reels, but Scott was delighted to find a print of the film that was closer to his original conception. Further screenings at the Academy of Motion Picture Arts and Sciences sold out well in advance, and enthusiasm for the alternative version was strong enough to tempt Warners into a 're-release' of a restored print. A 35mm version of the workprint was shown to steadily building audiences at the NuArt Theatre in Los Angeles and the Castro in San Francisco, where it broke box-office records.

At that point, Arick, Warners and Scott were all interested in preparing a more official re-release, a 'director's cut' of *Blade Runner* that would restore the film's original, darker, vision. Unfortunately, Scott was not insistent enough, and Warners not willing enough on its own, to rework the film as fully as was first intended. Nevertheless, the banal narration was scrapped, in its entirety this time; the ambivalent original ending was restored; and the 'unicorn reverie' was inserted in one scene (a different version from the one first filmed, because the original footage was probably destroyed). The version as finally released also contained numerous sound continuity errors, footage that hadn't been colour-corrected, and it lacked some of the more violent footage that had been part of the film's original international release version. While known as the Director's Cut, it was more of a compromise between the 1982 domestic release and the version originally envisioned by its director.

With the narration jettisoned, the film's formal opulence became more pronounced. As Deckard approaches police headquarters, the viewer is now free to contemplate the cityspace with him: to see what can be seen through the rain-spattered windscreen; to make connections between the hovercar's graphic displays and the real space through which it glides; ultimately, to read the space. Freed of the teleology of a narration that told more than it should, the viewer could become more fully engaged by *Blade Runner*'s elaborate scenography. Further, now that they could be heard, ambient sounds and advertising slogans ('Helping America into the new world!') enhanced the richness of the film's sonic texture and provided an effective analogue to the film's decentred scopic field.

(Overleaf) Know thy maker?

The Director's Cut was released in September 1992 to mark the tenth anniversary of the original release. With its grandeur restored to the scale of the big screen, *Blade Runner* was more gorgeous than ever, and audiences responded. Its opening weekend earned the highest per-screen revenues in the country, and the film continued to play in nearly one hundred cinemas a month later. This success continued in Europe, Japan and Australia. As Paul Sammon wrote, 'Not bad for a film that was already a decade old. Or which had previously gained such wide exposure on cable TV, laser disk, and home video.'[36] The reviews improved – William Kolb found that the film's average ratings rose half a star! – but the film was now immune to mainstream critical opinion.

Blade Runner acquired a reputation for coldness, but it contained some surprising and satisfying moments of intimate, sensual detail: the blood that flows from Deckard's wounded lip into his glass of vodka; Pris's tongue protruding from her dead lips as Batty caresses it with his. The film feels languid, like the wind chimes heard in some scenes. The score by Vangelis, more tonal than melodic, evokes a poignant melancholia. Sometimes the film even seems to be taking place underwater: reflections play off the walls, liquid sounds are exaggerated and in the final battle water drips down the walls of the Bradbury Building. Batty dies in the rain, speaking of what he's seen: 'Attack ships on fire off the shoulder of Orion. I watched c-beams glitter in the dark near the Tanhauser Gate. All those moments will be lost in time. Like tears in rain. Time to die.'

The *Blade Runner* Effect

The impact of *Blade Runner* continues to be felt. There has been a continuing movement beyond the original boundaries of the text, with comic-book adaptations, a series of sequels and the discussion groups and Web sites that proliferate on the Internet. In 1996, Paul Sammon's *Future Noir: The Making of* Blade Runner appeared, and the British Film Institute included the film as part of its canon of important films (resulting in the present volume). Is it any wonder that the film continues to exist beyond itself? Its very style already promised infinite expansion.

The aesthetic of cyberpunk was almost defined by *Blade Runner*, although both were anticipated by the comics of *Heavy Metal*. They had other sources in common as well, including the influence of *Electric Sheep*'s author. *Blade Runner* stimulated the rediscovery of Philip K. Dick – perhaps this was its most significant effect. Ironically, Dick had been asked to write a novelisation of the film adaptation of his own novel, but he turned down this 'opportunity' and insisted instead upon the re-release of *Do Androids Dream of Electric Sheep?* The novel, appearing under the film's title, has not been out of print since the film was released. Properties that had been optioned years earlier were put into production, resulting in *Total Recall* (1990) and *Screamers* (1995), based on Dick's stories 'We Can Remember It for You Wholesale' and 'Second Variety'. Both played with themes of appearance versus reality, and both were adapted by Dan O'Bannon, who once worked with Moebius on a proto-cyberpunk thriller called *The Long Tomorrow*.

The Philip Dick renaissance continued with the republication of his complete short stories, and Vintage Books's release of a handsome set of some of his best novels. Excerpts from Dick's darkly paranoid journals, known as the *Exegesis*, have been edited and published by Lawrence Sutin, who also wrote a biography of the author. All of this, of course, came too late for Philip Dick. In 1982, shortly after enthusiastically approving an early cut of *Blade Runner*, he died of a massive heart attack.

2 The Metropolis

Science Fiction in the City

Blade Runner reminds us that cinema, science fiction and modern urbanism were interwoven products of the same industrial revolution. The city as a monumental form has been mapped and remapped in science fiction, as both utopia and dystopia. While utopian aspirations were focused on agrarianism, the city was pictured as a negative space. In the late 19th century, beginning with Edward Bellamy's *Looking Backward* (1888), the urban utopia gained prominence, perhaps reaching its apotheosis in the visual science fiction of the 20s, including the superb cinematic cities of *Metropolis* (which has its utopian side) in 1926 and *Just Imagine* (1930), and in the pulp magazine artwork of Frank R. Paul, who

Pre-production artwork by Syd Mead

painted fabulous rococo images of new vehicles and engines for living.

The economic slump of the 30s produced more pragmatic utopias, dreams of technology as well as centralised planning. *Things to Come* (1936), directed by William Cameron Menzies from a script by H.G. Wells, featured the prototypical rationalist city of gleaming white. In the film, civilisation falls in a massive world war, only to rise again with Wells's technocratic elite, The Brotherhood of Efficiency. The

'Everytown' that they build on the ruins of the old is a machine-produced perfection, untouched by human hands. Streamlined and monumental, Everytown circa 2036 unintentionally diminished and overwhelmed the mere mortals within its walls.[37]

The alienation and dis-ease of American culture in the 50s, coupled with the postwar white flight from urban centres, yielded science fiction cities that were claustrophobic and isolating, outsized monadic structures sealed off from their surroundings. In Isaac Asimov's *The Caves of Steel* (1954) Earth's population lives underground, and *Foundation* (1951) introduces a planet-sized metropolis devoid of natural forms: these aspects recur in *Blade Runner*.

In more recent years, a different image of the city emerged, first distinguished by its boundlessness. The new city became both micro and

Artwork for
Metropolis

macrocosm: imploded yet still monumental, insistent upon its status as a 'total space'. But urban space had also become non-physical: it was constituted less by buildings and highways than by invisibly penetrating networks of satellites and terminals. Geography was losing its relevance in the face of the topographies of electronic culture: Raoul Vaneigem wrote in 1963: 'We are living in a space and time that are out of joint, deprived of any reference point or coordinate.'[38] The new urban image was somehow both totalising and beyond the power of vision. Science fiction proved adept at imagining this slippery spatiality: J.G. Ballard's early story, 'The Concentration City' (1957),[39] presented an urban terrain defined by an infinity of space, a multiplicity of surfaces: the city circled back upon itself in a closed feedback loop. The city-state had become *the cybernetic state*.

Frozen domesticity in *Things to Come*

A similar unbounded urbanism became popular in science fiction comics of the 70s and 80s, including Britain's *Judge Dredd* and Italy's *Ranxerox*. In the pages of *Heavy Metal*, Moebius (Jean Giraud) created influential images of concentrated cities that filled the frame with level upon level of urban sprawl. In 'The Long Tomorrow', the city lay below the planet's surface, a chaos of intersecting lines and layers. Nothing ordered this littered and cluttered morass of high and low technologies, this city without top, without bottom, without limits. The only constant was the view that revealed everything in a single glance; a view both panoramic and kaleidoscopic.[40] *Blade Runner*'s future Los Angeles quoted the crowded urbanism of Moebius. Street level was like the underworld, the underside of the gleaming perspectives of *Things to Come*.

Science fiction depends upon an impossible, totalising gaze: according to Fredric Jameson it functions through spatial description more than narrative action. This privileged vision of space, common to Asimov, Moebius, *Blade Runner* and beyond, exemplifies the totalising gaze of science fiction. Jameson has argued that in the detective fiction of Raymond Chandler the plot focuses our superficial attention 'in such a way that the intolerable space of Southern California can enter the eye laterally, with its intensity undiminished'.[41] What he calls a 'lateral perceptual renewal' is, I think, extended in science fiction, a genre grounded in the new 'intolerable spaces' produced by advanced technology. Again and again the narrative permits an encounter with complex spaces that then become susceptible to comprehension, intervention and control.

The shift from the expansionist and visible machineries of the industrial age to the invisible technologies of the information age created a representational crisis for the genre. The purpose of much science fiction in the 80s, especially cyberpunk, was to construct a new position from which humans could interface with the global, yet hidden, realm of data circulation; a new identity to occupy the emerging electronic realm. I call this new position *terminal identity*, which refers both to the end of the traditional subject and the emergence of a new subjectivity constructed at the computer station or television screen.[42]

Cyberspace is the term used to refer to the 'space' constituted by information technologies, whether presented as an actual physical space (*Tron*) or a metaphorical *sense* of space, like an extended, immersive computer interface (*Neuromancer*). The concept took on value just as the topos of the traditional city had been superseded. A 'new conception of the urban' had arisen that was 'no longer synonymous with locale',[43] but was defined by the invisible circulation of information permitted by telecommunications technologies.

Science fiction had long been involved in a conceptual and phenomenological 'writing' of new urban spaces, so if the 'nonplace urban realm'[44] was invisible, then 'cyberspace' would render it visible, legible and spatial. Spatial and *kinetic*: the experience of cyberspace always emphasised motion. Maurice Merleau-Ponty wrote that 'to conceive space, it is in the first place necessary that we should have been thrust into it by our body'.[45] Cyberspace only becomes 'real' space in William Gibson's novel *Neuromancer* when the hero 'jacks in' to it. As a concept, cyberspace recreated the possibility of spatial exploration, and so helped to create an engagement with the global data system.

In *Blade Runner*, urban space moves toward the condition of cyberspace, and this is especially clear when Deckard electronically inspects one of Leon's photos. This, first of all, transforms the status of the object. The frozen stillness of the photograph, its inactivity and emptiness, brings Hopper's alienated urban interiors to mind, but the setting also strongly resembles something by Vermeer. A sharp light illuminates the scene from the left side of the image, and a convex mirror plays with light, reflection and surface in ways that again recall Vermeer or van Eyck. Just as this scene's reflection on the status of the cinematic image locates hidden details in the depth of the mirror, so did both Vermeer and van Eyck include obscure painted reflections of themselves in their canvasses.[46] There is, indeed, a story to be read there. By electronically enhancing the photo with his computer, the surface of the image is penetrated. This inert object, a mere trace of the past, becomes multidimensional and is suddenly possessed of the present-tense modality of cinema. Deckard issues commands like a film director ('Track right. . . . Now pull back . . .') and the frozen moment of the photograph is granted a new temporality. A grid is overlaid on this field and measured co-ordinates regulate and guide the detective's movement across the terrain of externalised memory. The classic scene of searching a room for clues is now played out on a terminal. The screen, that frontier separating electronic and physical realities, becomes permeable; the space behind it, tangible. The sequence anticipates the narratives of *Tron* and *Neuromancer*, in which humans are more physically inserted into cyberspace. The sequence, with its fantasied control of the projected image, is a most hypnotic meditation on cinematic power.

The Dark City

The dark and crowded space of cyberspace as introduced and described in *Neuromancer* was punctuated by neon forms and corporate structures, and the aesthetic of *Blade Runner* demonstrates that it had obvious precursors. In cyberspace the density of the central, inner, city became

Outrunning punks and priests

an analogy for the dispersed matrices of information circulation and overload, while cyberspace itself presented an urbanism stripped to its kinetic and monumental essentials. Cyberspace exaggerated the disorienting vertigo of the city, but it also summoned a powerful controlling gaze. Critics of cyberpunk tended to emphasise its dystopian cityscapes, missing the dialectic between the two modes of mutually informing existence, urban and electronic. Urban space and cyberspace each enabled an understanding and negotiation of the other.

Blade Runner may have lacked a context when it was first released, which might explain why so few critics recognised its power, but the film's heavy metal vision strongly influenced the emerging form of cyberpunk. The genre even begins to look like an attempt to grapple with the issues raised – or focused – by the film. These issues were also isolated, the same year, in Fredric Jameson's first essay on post-modernism (the next, more extended attempt appeared two years later, in 1984, virtually coinciding with the appearance of *Neuromancer*). Jameson wrote that cyberpunk is 'henceforth, for many of us, the supreme *literary* expression if not of postmodernism, then of late capitalism itself'.[47] His comment reveals a salient truth: science fiction had, in many ways, prefigured the dominant issues of post-modern culture.

Cyberpunk provided *the* image of the future in the 80s. The real advent of the science fiction subgenre happened with the publication of William Gibson's *Neuromancer* in 1984, but it was anticipated by at least three films from 1982 that had a formative impact upon the cyberpunk ethos and aesthetic: *Videodrome*, with its hallucinatory mass-media *guignol*; *Tron*, most of which took place in a cyberspace *avant la lettre*; and *Blade Runner*, with its urban density and romantic alienation. Gibson has made no secret of *Blade Runner*'s impact on his work.

Unlike most science fiction with a strong emphasis on technology, cyberpunk presented its worlds from street level: a view from below. Bruce Sterling, a cyberpunk author, editor and polemicist, wrote that times had changed 'since the comfortable era of Hugo Gernsback, when

Science was safely enshrined – and confined – in an ivory tower. The careless technophilia of those days belongs to a vanished, sluggish era, when authority still had a comfortable margin of control.'[48] The subgenre rejected Wellsian fantasies of rational planning in favour of a lived science fiction set among the outlaws and hackers of the demimonde. 'The street finds its own uses for things,' went one of its most famous credos, while another anarchically proclaimed, 'Information wants to be free.' Gibson's Johnny Mnemonic rents the memory chips implanted in his head to gangsters needing secret data storage space – again, this is light-years from the streamlined visions of progress in earlier science fiction.

Cyberpunk, like the film noir from which it partly derived, was defined as much by its tone and attitude as by its icons and narrative structures. Its high-tech urban settings were congested and confusing, yet also exhilarating. Communications and information media defined its future, and information density defined its style. *Blade Runner*'s cyberpunk urbanism exaggerates the presence of the mass media, evoking sensations of unreality and pervasive spectacle: advertising 'blimps' cruise above the buildings, touting the virtues of the off-world colonies, and gigantic vid-screens dominate the landscape with images of pill-popping geishas. Mead wanted the pervasive Asian graphics to contribute to the overall visual density without being easily comprehensible – creating a 'pure visual composite' like the experience of Japan for Roland Barthes in *Empire of Signs* or the narrator of Chris Marker's film *Sans Soleil*.[49]

Blade Runner and related works owe much to the alienated spaces of Raymond Chandler and Ross MacDonald. Motifs are shared by both genres: the tension between social order and disorder; narratives centred on perception and spatial exploration; and, most significantly, an emphasis on decentred, threatening urban spaces. *Blade Runner* is exemplary on all points. The replicants pose a threat to social order by raising questions about the status of being. Deckard, the technologically enhanced detective/perceiver, sees, reads and explores an unsettled, chaotic environment. And in the film's intricate urbanism, the iconographies of science fiction and noir overlap.

The city in *Blade Runner*, with its rain-slicked Los Angeles streets, *faux*-forties fashions, private-eye plot and world-weary narration, derives plenty from noir. This is a *dark city* of mean streets, moral ambiguities and an air of irresolution. *Blade Runner*'s Los Angeles exemplifies the failure of the rational city envisioned by urban planners and science fiction creators, and it also recalls, by implication, the air of masculine crisis that undergirded film noir – witness Deckard's struggle to retain, or regain, his humanity. If the metropolis in noir was a dystopian purgatory, then in *Blade Runner*, with its flame-belching towers, it has become an almost literal Inferno.

Cyberpunk's world was divided into heavily corporatised spaces of

Making eyes

control (the state served a minimal role: does representative government still exist in *Blade Runner*'s future?) and the marginalised figures who served as the genre's romantic, post-alienated protagonists. Many cyberpunk narratives sent their 'heroes' – who were more likely to be motivated by self-interest than revolutionary ideals – on incursions against the corporate strongholds of power. As with noir, the story's settings mixed decadent sleaze with decadent opulence, drawing a narrative web of complex and cynical social interactions.

Jameson wrote that Chandler's narratives reflected an American desire for people to overcome their separation from one another: the detective served as an agent of connection. 'And this separation is projected out onto space itself: no matter how crowded the street in question, the various solitudes never really merge into a collective experience, there is always distance between them.'[50] In *Blade Runner*, this separation extends into the distance between the human and the non-human, the organic and the technological, the natural and the cultural.

The link between noir and cyberpunk was neither superficial nor coincidental, but was connected to those 'intolerable spaces', once *urban* and now *cyber*. The task of narrating urban alienation and separation now fell to the hybrid of crime fiction and science fiction that was cyberpunk.

J. F. Sebastian

Retrofitting can serve as a useful – and convenient – metaphor for *Blade Runner* as a whole. In the film, a noir narrative is retrofitted onto science fictional speculations about human definition and development. In other cyberpunk, noir was mapped onto the invisible spaces of electronic culture. Retrofitting could even be a metaphor for science fiction in general, since familiar characters and narratives ground its extrapolations. If the genre often combines speculation with an uncanny resistance to change, this can be understood as an unavoidable part of its retrofitted nature.

As a literary movement, cyberpunk ended almost as soon as it began, but its impact continues to be felt across a range of media and cultural phenomena. Its techno-surreal strategies permanently altered the representation of electronic technology. Ultimately, 'cyberpunk' became a subcultural label, referring now to hackers, electronic musicians, ravers and anyone else who professed to employ high technology (or its image) from the margins of society.

The Bright City

Despite the darkness that pervades it, it is worth considering the utopian face of this city; for although this is a hell where we would never want to live, it is also, as repeat viewers of the film can attest, a hell of a nice place to visit.

What if the success of the city as an environment was *not* a function of its rational efficiency? What if the value of the metropolis derived from its status as an *irrational* space? Rem Koolhaas has written of New York as a delirious space masquerading behind a rational façade of gridded streets and high technology. The modern city is so vast and complex that it eludes representation and exists beyond easy understanding. It is a site of impossible congestion, an endless multiplication of floors, buildings, blocks. Every skyscraper is a city within a city, every floor organised by its own potentially 'unprecedented combinations' in which all of history and human experience was available for reference and plunder. The unified functionalism of the modernist city was only an organising myth, according to Koolhaas, and indeed it existed more in fictions like *Things to Come* than it ever would, could, or perhaps should in Manhattan.

The real vocabulary of New York's architecture was anticipated by the bright city of Coney Island, which existed as a kind of experimental laboratory for Manhattan's future; its towers and spires were preparation for the skyscrapers of the next decades. Coney Island offered the fluidity of a permanent carnival: shape-shifting, displacement and informality were the rules of disorder (none of this was encouraged by the guardians of propriety, who preferred a more subdued seaside park).

For Koolhaas, Coney provided the key to decoding New York City's latent, pervasive irrationalism, its poetic vocabulary. I think that it fell to cinema to inherit and extend what he called the 'metaphoric planning' of the city that had originated with the amusement park. Cinema combined spatiotemporal solidity with metamorphic fluidity. It also documented and even liberated the ephemerality latent in the urban field. Cinema could represent and rethink the city without quantifying it; it emphasised congestion and lived experience.

Blade Runner is a crowded film about a crowded city, but in the irrational city, congestion is no problem: 'Not for a moment does the theorist intend to relieve congestion; his true ambition is to escalate it to such intensity that it generates – as in a quantum leap – a completely new condition, where congestion becomes mysteriously positive.'[51] Urban planners Raymond Hood and Harvey Wiley Corbett believed that 'people swarm to the city *because* they like congestion'.[52] Congestion provided the wealth of experience that Simmel valued so highly, and which only some could find overwhelming. Hood 'saw New York – its people and buildings crowded into every which way on an irregular non-gridlike grid, constantly shoved into instant closeups and surprising long-shot vistas – as an unending exercise in shifting perspectives as stimulation'.[53] The language here suggests that the city had already become its own image: amusement parks and picture shows – from *Manhatta* and *Man with a Movie Camera* to *Blade Runner* – gave order to all the 'shifting perspectives' while indulging their kaleidoscopic variety.

Koolhaas noted that Coney Island offered an intensification, rather than a suspension, of urban pressure.[54] Its fantastic architecture became 'the arrangement of the technological apparatus that compensates for the loss of physical reality',[55] and the *cinema* accomplishes something similar: if Manhattan insisted on the superficial order of gridded streets and regular blocks, then cinema, armed with montage and mobility, could cut across it. The sailors of *On the Town*, to take a musical example, are hardly restricted by New York's topography; the rhythm of 'New York, New York' produces a new 'creative geography', liberating and joyous. And the camera can, as it does in *Psycho*, wander up the sides of buildings, enter through chance windows and strip the city bare of its orderly façade. There are, after all, eight million stories in the naked city . . .

Panoramic Perception, Fractal Geographies

Blade Runner's incessant movement through urban space is closely aligned with what historian Wolfgang Schivelbusch dubbed 'panoramic perception'. With the rise of railway travel in the 19th century, vision was put in motion. The replacement of horsedrawn coach by speeding train transformed travellers into spectators, separated from the world by velocity, closed compartments and a sheet of glass. Attention had to shift from proximate objects to distant panoramas. Commodification was as important as speed: 'The customer was kept in motion; he traveled through the department store as a train passenger traveled through the landscape.'[56] Goods and citizens both circulated through the city; they were displayed and objectified. There was anxiety, too, about the inexorable grasp of merchant capitalism, as well as the train-traveller's sense of hurtling out of control in a speeding projectile. Withdrawal into numbed alienation provided some psychological protection: this perceptual mode was founded on separation, abundance, anxiety and alienation.

The equally complex pleasures of cinema, with its own emphasis on objects and movement, extended panoramic perception. *Blade*

(Opposite) Pris

Runner offers an urban experience of inexhaustible fluidity, endless passage and infinite perceptibility – *a utopian vision*, so to speak, as distinct from *a vision of utopia*. A beautiful and technically impressive sequence appears early in the film, during Deckard's flight in the police spinner. The panoramic shot of the city, seen through the windscreen from behind Gaff and Deckard, combined thirty-five separate elements. Twenty miniature buildings were matched to projected Syd Mead artwork and overlaid with multiple layers of travelling mattes, miniature vehicles of varying scales and motion-controlled camerawork.[57]

The viewer is presented with two distinct spaces in this shot. The first is the superbly detailed urban space that dominates the film, visible outside the spinner. The panorama is augmented by the second space, constituted by the data screens of the cockpit, which reveals the existence of an 'invisible' traffic corridor. An order exists to the movements of the city, even if that order is not always evident to the unaided eye. The shot, with all of its composed elements and brilliant synchronisation of views, permits a totalising gaze of impossible clarity. The viewer is given a privileged tour of a futurity that is richly layered, bewildering but still familiar. The total effect is one of scopic pleasure: the viewer sees and deduces how (and *that*) the future works.

For me, the sequence recalls the trolley ride in *Sunrise* (1927), perhaps the most profound expression of panoramic perception in the history of the cinema.[58] After nearly strangling his wife, the man begs for forgiveness, but in terror and grief she runs from lakeshore to woods, boarding an improbable city-bound trolley. He follows, and as they stand at the front of the moving car the world beyond the windows slides laterally past them (and us). They seem fixed and centred in space, while the world itself has become unmoored. The sequence speaks, with impossible eloquence, of separation and disconnection, even as this most literal of tracking shots links rural and urban spaces in a fluid continuum. Despite its evident solidity, the world takes on a hallucinatory mutability. Our attention is divided between their unspeaking trauma and the complexly shifting space beyond the windows; we are divided between alienation and exploration.

Some of the poignance comes from the inescapable sense of loss built into the very aesthetic of the shot. Whatever comes into view will just as surely be removed, to be replaced, and replaced again. Absence and distance structure the image. Leo Charney has located variations on this absence as fundamental to the fascination that cinema exerted on such philosophers and theorists as Henri Bergson, Walter Benjamin and Jean Epstein. Characteristically, 'cinema transformed the hollow present into a new form of experience, as the vacated present opened space for the viewer's activity. Experience arose in – was defined by and in – the space vacated by the present's movement away from itself.'[59] In *Sunrise*, the movement of the world past the fixed frame of the camera becomes a metaphor for cinematic experience, in which plenitude and loss coexist in an unresolved dance of marked but unfulfilled desires.

Compare this to that expansive hovercraft flight in *Blade Runner*. Again the world slides past the window, but now we luxuriate without reservation in the revelation of urban immensity and complexity. Special effects sequences are often about revelation rather than absence – they evoke presence. A further moment's reflection, though, demonstrates that *Blade Runner*, with its retrofitted future built on the debris of the past – a past which is our present – *does* insist on a sense of absence and separation not dissimilar to *Sunrise*. This is consistent with the thematic emphasis on the passing of human centrality. Does memory remain the residue of something now absent, or is it only a simulation, a false presence? Charney notes that 'if the present disappears, and thereby hollows out presence, this shift also hollows out the subject who constructs that presence'. Interestingly enough, the modernist, human, subject is hollow, while replicants, with their implanted memories and false photographs, are permitted a luxurious illusion of wholeness.[60]

Blade Runner's exploration of urban existence continues through its transformations of scale and perspective. The monumental headquarters of the Tyrell Corporation, for example (which owes something to British science fiction illustrators Angus McKie and Chris

Foss), is vast beyond normal human experience, and in fact the human
form is almost always missing from these intricate visions. The limitless
complexity of the film suggests some precepts of chaos theory, which
holds that chaotic systems are not random but complex, non-linear
systems produced through massively repeated, simple operations. New
dimensions lie between the dimensions of traditional mathematics:
fractal dimensions. The natural order is distinguished by intricate and
infinite fragmentation and by similarities across different scales – fractal
forms such as coastlines or cloud patterns reveal equal complexity at any
magnification, so 'a fractal is a way of seeing infinity'.[61]

Blade Runner reveals the city itself to be a complex, self-similar
space – a fractal environment. The panoramic camera panned *across* the
spaces of the city, but the fractal camera also tracks *through* endless

Deckard and
Rachael

levels of scale. The film begins with an extreme long shot of Los Angeles
that encompasses its undifferentiated industrial overgrowth in one
panoramic view. The next shot offers a fiery smokestack punctuating the
diabolical space, which is then reflected in a disembodied eye. The
camera penetrates the space, moving forward to locate the gigantic Tyrell
corporate headquarters (note its microchip design – another similarity
across scale). After a violent interlude with Leon and a blade runner, the

camera finds Deckard by submerging to street level where there are advertising blimps, neon signs, 'trafficators', futuristic attire and glowing umbrella handles. A streetside vendor uses an electron microscope, and now the drama becomes molecular. Later, Deckard's electronic inspection of a photograph transforms its visual field, and the two-dimensional space of the photograph becomes the more three-dimensional space of cinema. Infinite complexity structures urban reality; *Blade Runner* defines the city as fractal *geography*.

The Return of the Modernist City

The polyglot architecture of *Blade Runner*'s future urbanism challenges the dream of a rational, centrally planned city. This city is dispersed, boundless, heterogeneous. The only monument is run by a techno-

Death in the streets

corporation, rather than a benign technocracy. The white cities of *Things to Come* and the 1893 World's Fair, and the Futurama of the 1939 fair, have been replaced by a city of darkness, night, chaos and delirium. The final battle between Deckard and Batty takes place at the Bradbury Building, designed by George Wyman in 1893 and inspired by the technocratic rational vision of Bellamy's utopian novel, *Looking Backward*. In *Blade Runner*, the Bradbury Building is an empty space of burst pipes, decay and deterioration, its space made hallucinatory by the searchlights that constantly sweep past its windows.

The rejection of the modernist ethos of centralised control has led nearly every critic to link *Blade Runner* to the spatiality of post-modernism: a decentred, ahistorical pastiche. Depth disappears in post-modern aesthetics, and with it goes history, psychology and individuality: what remains is a cacophony of signs. Nothing can any longer distinguish between sign and referent, simulation and original – and anyway, there is no longer any reason to make the distinction.

Nevertheless it might be pertinent to regard *Blade Runner* as a more deeply *modernist* city film. Its citation of earlier urban forms does not seem to be the ahistorical pastiche that defined post-modern architecture and art, but represents, rather, a more deeply historicised restatement of fundamental modernist ideas of the city. Critics, myself included, have tended to see the film's disparate buildings as the mark of a post-modern sensibility, but heterogeneity and urban chaos are nothing new, after all. Cities of the modern period were as heterogeneous as they could make themselves (it was also unavoidable unless the old city was razed, as in *Things to Come*). Ann Douglas, referring to Manhattan architecture in the 20s, writes:

If the skyscrapers represented, as some said, Babel, the implications weren't all bad. Babel was a cacophony of different languages; so were the skyscrapers … [New York's] new architecture made itself the host for motifs and styles from widely diverse cultures, present and past. Zigzag designs from American Indian culture and angular geometric patterns from ancient

Babylon and Assyria and Africa contradicted and supplemented Gothic towers, gargoyles, and Art Deco ornamentation. Writing about The Skyscraper in 1981, Paul Goldberger calls it 'the art of grafting . . . historical forms onto modern frames'.[62]

The rational, planned city of efficient circulation and an International Style, perhaps epitomised by the designs of Le Corbusier, belonged to another modernism entirely. *That* modernism is indeed rejected by *Blade Runner*, while the modernist experience of the city described by Simmel, Benjamin and Kracauer – disordered, heterogeneous, street-level – is revisited and renewed. The camera glides through this futuristic urban space in ways that recall nothing so much as the cinema of the late 20s and early 30s: the 'city symphonies', as well as work by Busby Berkeley (*42nd Street*, 1933), F. W. Murnau (*Sunrise*, *The Last Laugh*, 1924), Paul Fejös (*Lonesome*, 1928; *Broadway*, 1929) and Fritz Lang (*Metropolis*). The city has existed in cinema as a place of delirious chaos, alienation, resistance and even improbable liberation. *This* city once again finds eloquent voice in *Blade Runner*.

Gotham City

'Gotham City' was one of Ridley Scott's original titles for *Blade Runner*, which suggests that we might need to rethink the significance of the film's Los Angeles setting. It has become a commonplace to note the transition from New York to Los Angeles as a site of utopian/dystopian projection, which is supposedly indicative of the shift from a modernist to a post-modernist aesthetic. The towering, and brand new, Empire State Building that King Kong climbed has been replaced by the boundless, retrofitted sprawl of *Blade Runner*. In John Carpenter's *Escape from New York* (1981), everybody wants out of the maximum security detention centre that Manhattan has become, while in *Escape from LA* (1996), folks are pretty content – 'I *looove* LA,' Pam Grier's transsexual character enthuses, among the ruins.

But *Blade Runner* is arguably as fundamentally a New York film as

Fritz Lang's *Metropolis*. Lang was inspired by New York's burgeoning skyline, the familiar tale goes, while on a 1924 tour promoting *Die Niebelungen*. His description evoked the city in all its kaleidoscopic glory: 'There are flashes of red and blue and gleaming white, screaming green ... streets full of moving, turning, spiraling lights, and high above the cars and elevated trains, skyscrapers appear in blue and gold, white and purple, and still higher above there are advertisements surpassing the stars with their light.'[63] *Wow!* Lang double-exposed his photographs to capture Broadway's kinetic lights. This might account for the continual seductiveness of *Metropolis* and its urban vision – the city remains a glittering toy, a place of endless possibilities despite the regimented, claustrophobic workers' city hidden below ground. In fact, J.P. Telotte has suggested that *Metropolis* is partly a meditation on the seductiveness of technology (in the forms of the robot Maria, the city itself and the film's own opulent effects).[64]

But all of this is equally true of *Blade Runner*; despite its ostensible and determining Los Angeles setting, it's possible to see the film as a return to the modernist urbanism exemplified by New York. 'The city we present is overkill. But I always get the impression of New York as being overkill,' Ridley Scott has said. 'You go into New York on a bad day and you look around and you feel this place is going to grind to a halt any minute.'[65] Syd Mead 'had the Manhattan skyline in mind while creating his original preproduction designs', and Scott wanted the Chrysler Building, a superb art deco icon, to figure prominently.[66] One critic noted the disparity between *Blade Runner*'s Los Angeles and the real one: Scott accomplished 'what generations of city planners have failed to do in reality: he has give Los Angeles a downtown. Horizontal LA has vanished into vertical New York.'[67]

And, to close the cinematic circle, special effects supervisor David Dryer has said, 'Someday I want to take shots from Fritz Lang's *Metropolis* and shots from *Blade Runner* and run them back to back. Because there's an awful lot of *Metropolis* in *Blade Runner*.' He added: 'I was even using stills from *Metropolis* when I was lining up *Blade Runner*'s miniature building shots.'[68] Affinities between *Metropolis* and *Blade Runner* are almost too numerous to mention, and the resemblance runs deep – *Blade Runner* doesn't just refer back to the earlier film, but to the very issues that dominated it.

Both films present the built, urban environment as a total space. Nature only appears in *Metropolis* in the form of roof gardens for the very wealthy. Similarly, *Blade Runner* presents a heavy trade in artificial animals, and in the original novel, apartment rooftops offer grazing areas for the surviving animals (or their synthetic replacements) – major status symbols. Both films establish a high/low dichotomy with the wealthy literally occupying the upper strata of society, while the workers struggle below. This industrial-era division of labour was announced in *The Time Machine* by H.G. Wells, with its distant future of leisure-loving humans and their subhuman slaves, the Morlocks.

The cities in *Metropolis* and *Blade Runner* are massive, but each is punctuated by a monumental building – the Stadtkrone Tower and the Tyrell Building, respectively. The tower in *Metropolis* is modelled on Brueghel's 1563 rendering of the Tower of Babel; the corporate headquarters of the later film quotes Mayan pyramids. In *Metropolis* we view the tower from below its apex, as its four points radiate control over the city, but in one of Erich Kettelhut's beautiful production drawings we look down on it from almost directly above, prefiguring *Blade Runner*'s gorgeous hovercraft approach to police headquarters (Ridley Scott had often arrived in Manhattan by helicopter, landing on the Pan Am Building).[69]

Metropolis was produced in the midst of an urban renaissance, and in the 20s New York skyscrapers with their relatively unadorned vertical thrust epitomised twentieth-century urbanism and capital accumulation. The gaze of the urban citizen was granted a kind of 'upward mobility'. *Blade Runner* recreates this gaze, but as a nostalgic return, not to the city as a centred and controlled environment, but to the city as a *cinematic* environment, an industrial space poeticised and narrated by the camera.

3 Replicants and Mental Life

Cinema and Synthetic Life

Before stories of synthetic humans were given over to the ostensibly rational worlds of technology and science fiction, they were the stuff of myth, fantasy, fairy tales and horror. And while mechanical automata never quite attained the idealised perfection of Olympia in Hoffmann's 'The Sandman', or the Edison-built Hadaly in *The Eve of the Future* (Villiers de L'Isle Adam, 1886), they had nonetheless astonished audiences and brought acclaim to their designers. In the 18th century, Vaucanson unveiled a mechanised excreting duck and a pump-operated flautist with mechanical fingers. The human body was a fabulously intricate mechanism, but it could be mimicked and perhaps even replicated. What, then, was the human?

In the late 19th century, another machine began generating a simulacrum of life – the cinema. Shadows took on volume and a real-time existence, their actions could move audiences to tears, laughter or anger. Uncle Josh, in a 1902 film by Edwin S. Porter (under the auspices of Edison, a recurring figure in this story), thinks the projected figures are real: like Hoffmann's Nathaniel, he tries to woo and win the silent simulation. Another early Edison film was an adaptation of *Frankenstein*, which would be refilmed in the early 30s. Now the monster was brought to life with electricity and light – the stuff of cinema. Around the same time, King Kong was being billed as the Eighth Wonder of the World, but did that refer to the giant ape or to the miniature one endowed with the image of life by animator Willis O'Brien? In *Pinocchio*, Gepetto, like the artisans of the Disney studio, wanted his crafted object to be 'a real boy'. Cinema not only creates life, it reflects upon that very desire.

Synthetic human narratives, from *Pygmalion* to *Pinocchio* to *Terminator 2*, have always challenged, or at least made explicit, definitions of 'natural' humanity and its role or function. Defining the human provides most of *Blade Runner*'s philosophical focus. Deckard gives empathy tests to suspected non-humans. Indeed, he might or might not be a replicant himself: 'How do you know you haven't retired a human by mistake?' Rachael asks him. 'Have you ever taken the test yourself?' In *Creation of the Humanoids* (1962), a terrific low-budget precursor to *Blade Runner* written and directed by Wesley Barry, humanoids are becoming disturbingly perfect simulacra. The protagonist is a member of the reactionary Order of Flesh and Blood, but he turns out to be a humanoid after all, and the other humanoids give him an operation to upgrade him to the new, sexually reproducing, model R100. 'Of course, the operation was a success,' the narrator assures us at the end, 'or *you* wouldn't be here.'

One more reason *Blade Runner* was seen as exemplary of post-modernism stemmed from its ambiguous attitude towards the replicants. 'For the cyberpunks,' Bruce Sterling proclaimed, 'technology is visceral

The serial image

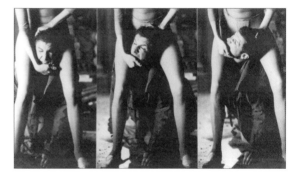

... [I]t is pervasive, utterly intimate. Not outside us, but next to us. Under our skin; often, inside our minds.'[70] Replicants melded technology and 'us': with their physical and mental, and perhaps emotional and erotic, superiority, they represented some fulfilment of Jean Baudrillard's discourse on simulation (and seduction) – the copy had superseded and even surpassed the original. Map replaced territory. The only important difference between humans and replicants was programmed: a four-year lifespan operates as a fail-safe mechanism, protecting the human from its own obsolescence.

Do Androids Dream of Electric Sheep?

The engagingly paranoid sensibility of Philip K. Dick explored the alienation that comes from seeing through simulations. His protagonists undergo personal crises as the boundaries between the real and the simulated begin to dissolve. But these aren't just isolated psychotic breakdowns; they follow from the expansion of technologies of reproduction (television and computers, for example) and the rising incidence of simulation in the so-called 'real world'. In Dick's fiction, social intercourse with imitation humans replaces involvement with real ones. Entrepreneurs market famnexdo (family-next-door) units to lonely interplanetary colonists so they'll have neighbours. Advertisements are annoying little fly-sized robots. Disillusioned, isolated Martian colonists take a drug and enter the 50s suburban dream-world of Perky Pat.

Roy

A corporate mogul employs staff to provide authentic items from his youth: props in a huge simulacrum that he uses as a retreat. Teaching machines dispense information and kindly wisdom: interacting with them is like watching television, only more so. Again and again, spectacles usurp reality.

Around the same time, the political philosopher and artist Guy Debord proclaimed that reality was dissolving into mass media 'spectacle', adding that 'the spectacle originates in the loss of unity of the world'.[71] '[T]he spectator feels at home nowhere, because the spectacle is everywhere.'[72] The schizophrenia that characterises so many of Dick's 'heroes' is possibly a reasonable response to an insane world. In *Blade Runner* and its source novel, the confusion between human and non-human pervades the world: objects like traffic lights and billboards talk to everyone all the time. Dick once remarked: 'The ultimate in paranoia is not when everyone is against you but when every*thing* is against you. Instead of "My boss is plotting against me," it would be "My boss's *phone* is plotting against me."'[73]

In *Do Androids Dream of Electric Sheep?* androids (or andys) are given as incentives to encourage emigration to the off-world colonies, but since they don't like it out there any more than the humans do, they

Among toys

keep making their way back to Earth. The San Francisco where the action occurs is a site of decay: emotional, physical and bodily. Citizens dial up desired emotions (for example, 'The desire to watch TV no matter what's on') on their 'mood organs' and experience an ersatz empathy with a virtual religious martyr. Humans, then, are as programmed with false feelings as their android enemies.

Electric Sheep is Dick's most sustained exploration of the 'nature' of the non-human. Androids emphasise the definition of the human by displacing mere biology as the sole, sufficient, condition. The underlying issue is not whether we can give a machine the qualities of the human, but whether the human has lost its humanity; whether it has become, in fact, a machine. In writing *Electric Sheep*, Dick had been thinking of the Third Reich: 'With the Nazis, what we were essentially dealing with was a defective group mind, a mind so emotionally defective that the word "human" could not be applied to them.'[74] There is much less opportunity for identification with the replicants in the novel than in the film, as Dick pointed out:

To me, the replicants are deplorable. … They are essentially less than human entities. … Ridley, on the other hand, said he regarded them as supermen who couldn't fly. He said they were smarter, stronger and had faster reflexes than humans. 'Golly!' that's all I could think of to reply to that one. I mean, Ridley's attitude was quite a divergence from my original point of view, since the theme of my book is that Deckard is dehumanized through the tracking down of the androids.[75]

Here Dick protests a bit too much. In fact, his text is inconsistent, shifting scene by scene, with the androids taking on the role of victims at some points and of villains at others. Nevertheless, the theme of dehumanisation is central to *Electric Sheep* and to most of Dick's prodigious output.

Philip Dick gives us two oppositions: Human/Android and Human/Inhuman. The first is ultimately unimportant, while the second is urgent. The division between human and android raises a central philosophical question: how do you *know* you're human? The second opposition leads to a moral problem: what does it *mean* to be human? If some post-modern theorists and artists would reject the relevance of this second question, finding in it a nostalgic and outmoded humanist attitude, there should be no doubt that this is what lies at the centre of his work.

In the world as defined by Philip K. Dick, the human is that which experiences empathy (by contrast, in the work of Isaac Asimov, adaptable intelligence is the determining factor). But if androids have no feelings, then it's worth noting that blade runners are not supposed to feel anything (hatred, fear, lust) for their victims. In the novel, Deckard confidently locates the difference between humans and their imitations: 'An android doesn't care what happens to another android,' to which someone logically replies, 'Then you must be an android.'

The novel and the film are filled with tests: there are tests to determine who's human, who's fit to reproduce, who's fit to emigrate. The obsession with boundaries, definitions and standards indicates that these definitions are in crisis. In Dick's novel, the Voight-Kampff scale measures empathic response – but there is discussion that human schizophrenics, those suffering from a 'flattening of emotional affect', would also fail the test. But R.D. Laing and, later, Fredric Jameson and others have argued that our whole post-modern culture inculcates a 'waning of affect' and that 'schizophrenia' is an increasingly common and even appropriate response. In a post-modern world of mass media, spectacle and simulation, it becomes increasingly difficult to tell the difference between humans and replicants ...

Blade Runner performs an ingenious variation on the definitions of humanity that dominated science fiction film in the 50s: in *I Married a Monster from Outer Space*, *The Thing from Another World*, *Invaders from Mars* or *Invasion of the Body Snatchers*, humans simply have feelings while non-humans simply do not. *Blade Runner* denaturalises that division and subtly inverts it: *what has feelings is human*. Thus the film is as much about Deckard's recovery of empathic response as it is about Batty's development of such a response.

The Human/Android division, then, is the narrative vehicle for the deeper and more urgent distinction to be made between Human and Inhuman. The science fiction writer and critic Norman Spinrad has put it elegantly:

What ultimately makes the androids in *Do Androids Dream of Electric Sheep?* less than human is not their synthetic origin, but like the Nazis in *The Man in the High Castle*, their lack of *caritas*, their inability to empathize with the existential plight of other life forms caught in the same multiverse. What raises the android Roy Batty to human status in *Blade Runner* is that, on the brink of his own death, he is able to empathize with Deckard. What

Dolls

makes [Dick's protagonists] true heroes is that ultimately, on one level or another, whatever reality mazes they may be caught in, they realize that the true base reality is not absolute or perceptual, but moral and empathetic ...[76]

Simmel wrote that a sense of 'reserve' is necessary to surviving in the city: 'the metropolitan type ... creates a protective organ for itself against the profound disruption with which the fluctuations and discontinuities of the external milieu threaten it'.[77] Replicants, supposedly lacking emotions and empathy, are thus exemplary city dwellers. Capitalist relations encourage rational rather than emotional reactions, but doesn't an attitude of 'formal justice' combined with 'unrelenting hardness' describe blade runners at least as much as their adversaries?

The unicorn

Effective blade runners won't – *can't* – acknowledge any resemblance between replicant and human. Empathy, for a blade runner, would make it impossible to function; that 'reserve' must be kept in place. Upon meeting Rachael, who thinks she's human, Deckard confronts her manufacturer: 'How can it not know what it is?' He falls in love with her, but in an unfilmed scene another blade runner tells him: 'You might as well go fuck your washing machine.' Simmel understood this defensive and ultimately self-defeating reaction: 'We see that the self-preservation of certain types of personalities is obtained at the cost of devaluing the entire objective world, ending inevitably in dragging the personality downward into a feeling of its own valuelessness.'[78] *Blade Runner* takes place at what must be the end of this process, with a humanity that has been dragged downward and devalued.

Deckard must learn to regard the replicants as more than mere commodities. J.F. Sebastian, a genetically defective designer for the Tyrell Corporation, already exists somewhat outside the cycle of pervasive commercialism, and he resembles Gepetto more than a capitalist tycoon. For him, synthetic life forms provide companionship: 'I *make* friends', he tells Pris, referring to his playful automata (and incidentally providing a perfect illustration of science fiction's playful language).

New Bodies for New Worlds

When they meet, Roy Batty tells Sebastian, 'We're not computers... we're *physical*.' The robot, android, replicant and cyborg are technological selves that are really correlates of century-old technological anxieties. Wolfgang Schivelbusch reminds us of the *trauma* of industrialisation, exemplified by industrial accidents:

It must be remembered that railway accidents have this peculiarity, that they come upon the sufferers instantaneously without warning, or with but a few seconds for preparation, and that the utter helplessness of a human being in the midst of the great masses in motion renders these accidents peculiarly terrible.[79]

The merely human body wasn't designed for the stresses and shocks of a mechanical world. The body had to be armoured against modernity. Superheroes appeared on the American industrial landscape in the 30s – the Man of Steel had the right stuff to exist in the Machine Age. As embodied by the new bodies of superheroes, robots or replicants, the 'utter helplessness of the human being' could be overcome – technological trauma produced its own antidote; or, as the poster for *Blade Runner* put it, 'Man has made his match ...'.

In cyberpunk fantasies of technological symbiosis, control of one's self was actually enhanced by the body's disappearance either into cyberspace or cyborg forms. The dissolution of the body, and its replacement by its own technological simulation, was repeatedly posited as *empowering*. Technology was internalised, bound to a sense of self that was strengthened but which somehow remained basically the same.

Donna Haraway redefined the value of the cyborg in ways that are more relevant to *Blade Runner*'s ambiguities. In her well-known 'manifesto for cyborgs' she argued for a feminist rereading of technological being in a world that has blurred distinctions between organism and machine. This is a 'border war' with high stakes: 'Our machines are disturbingly lively,' she noted (and this is Deckard's problem in a nutshell), 'and we ourselves frighteningly inert.'[80] The cyborg has some advantages for a feminist (or otherwise radical) politics: first of all, it can't be regarded as *natural*. The dualisms that structure too much Western thought can be supplanted through a cyborg mythology: 'A cyborg body is not innocent; it was not born in a garden; it does not seek unitary identity and so generate antagonistic dualities without end (or until the world ends); it takes irony for granted.'[81] Just as Michel Foucault declared: 'man is only a recent invention, a figure not yet two centuries old, a new wrinkle in our knowledge; he will disappear again as soon as that knowledge has discovered a new form'.[82] For Haraway, we are all 'theorized and fabricated hybrids of machine and organism; in short, we are cyborgs'.[83] Her 'cyborg politics' opens the idea of technological symbiosis as a dynamic exploration, not just a masculine fantasy of 'natural' mastery and domination over nature, technology and 'others'. Rather than static armoured bodies of the Schwarzenegger variety, Haraway's cyborgs are fluid, active participants in the making or remaking of their selves and their culture.

New Selves

Blade Runner appeared just as issues of identity – bodily anxiety and broader tensions around gender, race and subjective experience – were making themselves felt in popular culture. In science fiction, which was becoming increasingly central to mass culture, aliens, cyborgs and androids played out a range of identity-constructions and formations. Within the fractal geographies of *Blade Runner*, the 'human' was increasingly open to question. What was human, and what in the world could it do in this world?

In many ways, of course, the film is very traditional (that is, reactionary) regarding gender and racial politics. Critics, Andrew Ross prominent among them, have concentrated exclusively upon the film's demonstrable anxiety over urban ethnic pluralism. Harrison Ford's Rick Deckard becomes an archetypal alienated white male battling his way through – and, in the original release, out of – an extended inner-city ghetto environment (Ford has made a career out of playing such action figures, including Indiana Jones, Han Solo and Jack Ryan, although without the bizarre masochism one finds in the work of Michael Douglas). There is clearly something to this reading of the film's racial politics, especially in relation to its representation of Asians. In the early 80s, the expanding economic influence of Japan yielded waves of hysterical racism in the United States, and *Blade Runner* and (even more) Ridley Scott's next film, *Black Rain*, and Michael Crichton's *Rising Sun* are products of that moment. Further, a more generalised urban paranoia did find a voice in cyberpunk, as well as in many of the so-called 'action-adventure' films of the 80s and 90s. Both of John Carpenter's *Escape* films seem like simple white-revenge movies (especially in *Escape from LA*, when Snake, our hero, sinks a full-court shot and the black, Asian and Chicano crowd goes wild). *Blade Runner*, however, is more complicated, and to stop the analysis of the film's racial imagery at this point is to ignore significant parts of the film's metaphorical system.

There is an acutely embarrassing moment in the original release of *Blade Runner* in which Deckard characterises his boss as someone who would once have used the word 'nigger' to describe blacks. The word hangs in the air of the movie theatre, ugly and over-obvious; quite out of keeping with the world of 'replicants', 'blade runners' and the film's other neologistic creations. The idea of racial prejudice is still central to the film, although not as explicitly as in that voice-over, nor as much as in Dick's original. In the book, an advertisement for androids promises to 'duplicate the halcyon days of the pre-Civil War Southern states!' These 'custom-tailored humanoid robots' could serve as 'tireless field hands', the ad suggests. *Blade Runner* preserves Dick's analogy, as well as the 'passing narrative' of escaped slaves that underlies the novel. Replicants are passing for human rather than for white, but at one time, of course, blacks were not 'defined' as human by American slave-holding interests.

    Kaja Silverman has offered a compelling interpretation of the racial elements in the film, arguing that the metaphor of the replicants

Gaff

repositions slavery as a state of political being rather than a racial, and therefore natural, condition. Rutger Hauer's Roy Batty might look like a poster child for the Aryan Nation, but as the leader of the slave rebellion he actually becomes the deepest embodiment of 'blackness' in the film – Silverman argues that his 'hyperbolic whiteness' separates slavery and race, while also displacing the white male human from his normally privileged position within such hierarchies.

So, if on one level *Blade Runner* plays to traditional perceptions of race, it also manages to confound simple definitions and distinctions. Again, the more deeply one penetrates the opulent visual surface, the more unstable categories and meanings become. This extends to the film's overall treatment of gender issues, which are more complex here than in Dick's novel. All three of the major female characters are replicants (two are shot in the back by the panicky Deckard). Replicants are not permitted to compete with humans – their four-year lifespan artificially tilts the playing field – they're not even allowed to exist on this planet. So the replicants are doubly marginalised, aligned with cultural definitions of 'black' and 'woman' – they are doubly defined as victims within the constructs of Western culture. But once again the film refuses simply to 'naturalise' its victims as either women or blacks – Roy is as hyperbolically male and heterosexual as he is hyperbolically white. What defines the replicants as victims is the status they're given; it is their treatment by humans, and nothing inherent about 'them', that makes them who and what they are. As far as being 'human' goes, they are simply defined right out of existence. This is common in synthetic human narratives; it's central to Mary Shelley's *Frankenstein* and Lerner and Loewe's *My Fair Lady*, to name two.

There is, incidentally, an additional ironic reversal: replicants supposedly lack empathy, linking them not to the feminine but to masculine rationality, self-control and willing repression (like *Star Trek*'s Mr Spock). And yet from the first scene, in which Leon squares off against an annoyingly smug blade runner, the emotional life of the replicants clearly exists, and they continue to demonstrate ample empathy, at least for one another, as the narrative progresses. They are not just physically and intellectually superior to humans; in the dehumanised world that *Blade Runner* presents, replicants are 'more human than human', just as Tyrell proclaims. Their inferior status is arbitrary, solely a function of legal definition and the 'fail-safe mechanism' of a severely restricted lifespan.

Making History

Science fiction describes the commodification of *memory*, which can produce an ersatz humanity. In Trumbull's *Brainstorm*, recorded sensory experiences can be sold – a consumer can 'jack in' to a range of virtual activities. When its inventor discovers that it also records memories, he prepares a tape for his estranged wife. 'What is it?' she asks, and he

Fugitive

simply answers: 'Me.' In 'Overdrawn at the Memory Bank,' by John Varley (1976), citizens can store their memories as a hedge against future bodily catastrophe. In an era of bodily transformation, change and dissolution, the fact of physical existence doesn't guarantee selfhood. *Memory* becomes constitutive of the self – its continuity implies a kind of immortality, and the vicissitudes of the flesh become irrelevant.

Replicants are programmed with memories to make them indistinguishable from humans. They've been given photographs, visual totems of these artificial memories. 'Photographs are essentially history,' Ridley Scott noted, 'which is what these replicants don't have.'[84] The tangibility of the photograph creates a substitute history that belies the replicants' artificial origins. Photos nail things down – reality, identity, history – because we believe them to be fundamentally connected to

what they depict. Somehow, the light reflecting from a body has been fixed on paper and reaches out to my eye in the present moment. Roland Barthes describes it this way: 'A sort of umbilical cord links the body of the photographed thing to my gaze.'[85] A provocative image to consider alongside *Blade Runner*, a film fairly obsessed with mothers ('Let me tell you about my mother . . .'). When Deckard looks at a photo of Rachael with her mother it seems to flicker briefly to life, like the

A vertiginous outlook

central image in Chris Marker's time-travel reverie, *La Jetée* (1964).
Did it really happen? Did it *ever* happen?

It's important to remember, however, that memories are not givens,
even for humans – we select, distort and misremember. Our pasts are, to
some extent, constructions; so then are our selves. In a discussion of
memory, the neurologist Oliver Sacks quotes an article from 1956, 'On
Memory and Childhood Amnesia', by Ernest G. Schachtel:

> Memory as a function of the living personality can be understood only as a
> capacity for the organization and reconstruction of past experiences and
> impressions in the service of present needs, fears and interests. ... Just as
> there is no such thing as impersonal perception and impersonal experience,
> there is also no impersonal memory.[86]

Sacks himself has written a
case-study of a man who could
not hold anything in his
memory for any length of time,
and so had to remake his life
from moment to moment.
Sacks cites Luis Buñuel on the
necessity of memory: 'Life
without memory is no life at all.
... Our memory is our
coherence, our reason, our
feeling, even our action.
Without it, we are nothing.'
Sacks asks what can be done
for such patients. 'Can we
create a time-capsule, a
fiction?'[87] This is, in effect,
exactly what the Tyrell
Corporation has done for its

Hunting the hunter

Nexus 6 replicants – created a fiction of time and history, and encapsulated it in the form of photographs.

Blade Runner both over and undervalues vision. Its own meticulous, shifting visuals mesmerise and convince, but the images *in* the film are not so reliable. The inescapable photographs that show up throughout *Blade Runner* are constantly being handled and flipped over, which emphasises their equally inescapable flatness and depthlessness. Memories are no more indelible than the paper a photograph is printed on; history is devalued as a guarantor of truth, stability and unified meaning. Photographs are constantly invoked as signs, but they are ultimately empty signs, signifiers of nothing.

As *synthetic* humans, replicants inherently challenge essentialist notions of identity. Identity stands revealed as a construction, the result of conscious or unconscious social and physical engineering. The last line of one of Fancher's scripts has Deckard reminiscing about his relationship with the 'retired' Rachael: 'I guess we made each other real,' he complacently reflects. But the value of *Blade Runner* as it exists, along with so much of Philip Dick's work, is that it makes us *un*real – we are forced, or at least encouraged, to confront our own constructedness, and by confronting our selves, to remake them.

Is Deckard a Replicant?

This point is perhaps missed by all those who need to determine Deckard's status – sometimes it seems that the question, 'Is Deckard a replicant?' has generated more discussion on the Internet than the existence of God. I would argue that asking the question is more important than determining the answer (and, further, that it's not about Deckard, it's about *us*). According to the film's editor, Terry Rawlings, 'Ridley himself may have definitely felt that Deckard was a replicant, but still, by the end of the picture, he intended to leave it up to the viewer to decide whether Deckard was one.'[88] But it is true that the various permutations of *Blade Runner*, a film, after all, of exquisite and careful visual touches, have made this a mystery to consider.

The crisis regarding Deckard's status is more pronounced in the novel than in the film adaptation, as when Deckard tries to call police headquarters and finds no record of his supervisor, his office or himself. Are these implanted memories? At one point, everyone is testing everyone else's status, and the reader has no idea 'who' knows what about 'whom'. Novel and film sustain this ambiguity towards Deckard: is he human or replicant? Some references are joking and suggestive, rather than definitive. Leon, who as we know only has a four-year lifespan, asks, 'How long will I live?', but he's going to kill Deckard *now*: 'Longer than you!' he snarls.

In the Director's Cut, without the backup of the retrospective, reassuring narration, Deckard emerged as a character of greater complexity. Where his laconic explanations had once placed him somewhat above the fray, in the Director's Cut he is clearly on the edge from the start. He has quit the force: 'retiring' replicants has no appeal. His panic in the face of the superhuman Nexus 6 replicants is a logical extension of the anxiety that now marks his character throughout. His status as a human – physically, psychically, morally – is increasingly in doubt. He is, quite simply, *out of control*. No retrospective, reassuring voice-over could disguise that any longer.

While it was pursued less emphatically here than in the novel, there were continual hints that Deckard might be something other than human. What, for example, of the blade runner who meets his demise in the film's opening scene? Is it a coincidence that he looks and sounds remarkably like Harrison Ford/Rick Deckard? Or are they the same model of blade runner? Isn't it odd that the headquarters of the Tyrell Corporation and Deckard's apartment (modelled on Frank Lloyd Wright's Ennis-Brown House of 1923) are both inspired by Mayan architectural design?[89] Why do Deckard's eyes briefly glow with a red reflection? And how does Gaff know about Deckard's unicorn reverie? Small wonder, then, that Deckard is edgy from the start, and that his anxiety so easily slides into paralysis and panic.

The Deckard debate is, in some ways, a denial of what the film really does offer, which is a double reading: undecidability. Noël Carroll has argued that *Citizen Kane* was designed to support two entirely contradictory interpretations of Rosebud's importance to Charles Foster Kane.[90] This is somewhat true of *Blade Runner* as well: Marvin Westmore, the film's chief makeup artist, noted that 'a lot of things we did on *Blade Runner* were "possibly it's this" or "possibly it's that"', in keeping with Scott's desire to make a film that was more evocative than explicit.[91] To some extent, though, Deckard's status is undecidable because nobody finally decided. Some versions of the script made Deckard into an android, others don't even raise the question. Scott wanted to include hints that Deckard was a replicant, but with all the changes and revisions, it's no wonder that audiences were baffled.

One might argue that in the original release, Deckard isn't a replicant, but in the Director's Cut, he is. Paul Sammon, the author of the definitive 'making-of' book on the film, 'deduces' that in the Director's Cut, 'Rick Deckard is a replicant'.[92] The answer lies, as it does for others, in Deckard's 'unicorn reverie', which may connect to the origami unicorn that Gaff later leaves in Deckard's hallway. According to the *Blade Runner* FAQ (Frequently Asked Questions) list on the Internet: 'Gaff left the unicorn outside Deckard's apartment because he knew that Deckard dreamt of a unicorn. If Gaff knew what Deckard was dreaming, then we can assume that Deckard was a replicant himself, and Gaff knew he would be dreaming of a unicorn.' In other words, the unicorn image was implanted, and Gaff knew it.

But the, to my mind, obsessive desire to answer the question has always seemed misguided. If Deckard *is* a replicant, then what's the moral of this story? The issue of human definition is clearly – to me – central to the work, and thus the *ambiguity* is crucial. Many of the clues to Deckard's status could certainly be taken metaphorically. The unicorn, for example, could easily represent Rachael: it *is*, after all, an archetype. Murray Chapman's FAQ reasonably links it to the unicorn symbolism in Tennessee Williams's *The Glass Menagerie*, and the girl who was 'different to other horses'. 'Rachael is (and always will be) a replicant among humans, and will be different, like a unicorn among horses, because of her termination date.' And when Rachael asks Deckard whether he has ever taken the Voight-Kampff test, she may not be asking about his literal human status, but about his capacity for the empathy that the machine measures.

On the other hand, for Slavoj Žižek, philosopher and cultural theorist, the most radical implications of *Blade Runner* depend upon Deckard's standing revealed as a replicant. *Blade Runner*, he argues, is valuable in that it stages a confrontation with our own 'replicant-status'. Žižek is writing through the discourse of Lacanian psychoanalysis, in which the self *never* belonged as fully to itself as Descartes's cogito implied or as fully as we want it to (Deckard and Descartes are homophones, he notes, a pun for which I'd give Philip Dick full credit). 'Our' replicant-status is not just a function of our constructedness (old news, really), but of the awareness of the *void* (the gap between 'our' and 'selves') that follows its recognition. It is the replicants' obvious knowledge of their own manufacture that makes them our (or Žižek's) 'impossible fantasy-formation'.[93]

Even before the advent of what is known as 'the society of the spectacle' the cogito was incomplete, but the exteriorisation of memory in the information age makes that fundamental error all the more evident. Computer networks and satellite systems make the 'decentred' or 'virtual' self newly unavoidable, but they hardly invented it.[94] Replicants expose the hubristic self-misconception of the human – the mythos of the self-sustaining 'self' becomes all the more untenable. Žižek writes: 'It is only when … I assume my replicant-status' that 'I become a truly human subject.'[95] It is when we acknowledge our own replicant-status that we come face to face with ourselves as that irresolvable paradox: the 'thing' that 'thinks'.[96]

Masquerading in the City

Žižek has criticised the Director's Cut as inadequate and compromised regarding Deckard's status. He *wants* Deckard to be unambiguously a replicant and to confront that reality: for him it is in that confrontation that the film's meaning lies. But there is someone else at the film's centre who *does* confront his post-human condition – *gleefully* – and while Deckard/Descartes remains mired in agonised denial, Roy Batty (batty, nutty, kooky) is romping through the film, the 'thing' that thinks and fights and pouts and plays and poses. More human than human, right? Batty provides a kind of antidote to Deckard's panicky blandness. After killing Tyrell, Batty rides the elevator back down the side of the pyramid. In one of the film's best subjective moments, he gazes heavenward in what Hampton Fancher points out is 'the only shot in the whole movie where you see stars. And they're moving away from him, as if he's some kind of fallen angel.'[97]

Roy is a perfect denizen of the modern city; he embodies its kaleidoscopic essence. The city, after all, is a masked ball, a place of emergence and submergence, opulent display and clandestine transformation. Criminals might benefit from the possibilities the concentrated city offered for anonymity, but they weren't alone. 'In retrospect it is clear that the laws of the costume ball have governed Manhattan's architecture,' Rem Koolhaas has claimed. 'The costume ball is the one formal convention in which the desire for individuality and extreme originality does not endanger collective performance but is actually a condition for it.'[98]

Rutger Hauer's fabulously campy performance turns Roy into a figure of resistance and play. 'Gosh … you've got a lot of great toys here,' he tells Sebastian, his voice quivering with lust. He exhibits real *joie de vivre* ('I want more life, *fucker*'), but demonstrates even more joy in *performance.* He purses his lips, taunts, teases, confesses remorse, paints his face and in general eroticises the world. In a few drafts of Fancher's screenplay, Roy's appearance in the final battle is described as being 'somewhere between a Comanche warrior and a transvestite'.[99] He jumbles male and not-male, white and not-white, human and not-human.

The protracted battle between Deckard and Roy extends from

Sebastian's home to other apartments in the near-abandoned Bradbury Building to the rooftops. Throughout this penultimate sequence there is a constant straining upward, a physicality reminiscent of the final showdown with the spider in *The Incredible Shrinking Man* (1957). There, too, the scenario forces the protagonist upwards in a straining gesture towards human triumph over an anti-human enemy: these are climbs towards transcendence. But *Blade Runner* will complicate these oppositions. Roy's death was the last sequence to be filmed, and while the exhaustion on Harrison Ford's face as he watches his 'enemy' die is real enough, it is also the exhaustion of humanity on display.

The only sign of transcendence that the Director's Cut provides is the shot of the dove that soars skyward at the point of Roy's death: easily the most banal image in the film. One problem with the shot is that Roy is hardly a transcendent figure; he is transgressive, and never more so than in that prolonged battle as the prey assumes the role of the hunter. Roy becomes, first of all, a kind of homophobic nightmare: Deckard's panic grows beyond rational bounds as lesions appear on Roy's skin and his beauty begins to decay. And Roy manages to track Deckard from room to room, from floor to ceiling, and even through walls and across abysmal gaps: as with the moving cameras of urban cinema, Roy transgresses the given topographies of urban space.

The city is a site for masquerade, a metamorphic zone, a place to disappear and reappear. The performative side of Roy Batty breaks down traditionally drawn distinctions between the authentic and the artificial, or theatrical, and is easily aligned with Richard Dyer's discussion of a similar dissolve in gay response to the musical.[100] Batty is fighting for his life, but it's his choice to transform that battle into a form of deadly play. It becomes an opportunity to slide from one persona to another, a *performance of self* that becomes an implicit challenge to Deckard's stoic desire to preserve the 'real'. The replicant's identity is surely real, but it's also as metamorphic as the urban space through which he moves.[101] The fluid positionality of *Blade Runner*'s urbanism is matched by Roy's equally fluid personality.

Conclusion

The ultimate relevance of *Blade Runner* lies in its doubled, complex understanding of what it must mean to be human, not only at the end of the 20th century, but throughout it. Slavoj Žižek refers to 'the eternal gnawing doubt over whether I am truly human or just an android – it is these very undecided, intermediate states which make me human'.[102] The urban environment becomes the place to become human or in-human. In Simmel's writing, a conflict exists in the metropolis between the human defined as a mere object of economic relations and the human as a unique and independent being. 'It is the function of the metropolis to make a place for the conflict,' he wrote.[103]

Perhaps *Blade Runner* only works as an effective extension of Simmel's thesis because of a post-modern nostalgia for a lost image of urban complexity: even congestion and alienation could be preferred to the disappearance of real public space and human bodies. But I suspect that Simmel's argument continues to be relevant because cities, at least images and stories of cities, continue to represent the human position within a still-increasingly technologised, commodified world. City films and urban science fictions like *Blade Runner* 'make a place' in which to test the tensions, and play out the contradictions, of concentrated cities, spectacular societies and the continuing struggle to exist in the bright dark spaces of the metropolis.

Notes

1 Fredric Jameson, *Postmodernism, or the Cultural Logic of Late Capitalism.* (Durham, NC: Duke University Press, 1991), p. 285.

2 See, for example, 'About 5,750 Words', in *The Jewel-Hinged Jaw: Notes on the Language of Science Fiction* (Elizabethtown, NY: Dragon Press, 1977), pp. 39–49, and *Starboard Wine: More Notes on the Language of Science Fiction* (Elizabethtown, NY: Dragon Press, 1984).

3 See, for example, 'Narrative Space', in *Questions of Cinema* (Bloomington: Indiana University Press, 1981), p. 44.

4 Brooks Landon, *The Aesthetics of Ambivalence: Rethinking Science Fiction in the Age of Electronic (Re)Production* (Westport, CT: Greenwood Press, 1992), p. 94.

5 'Ridley Scott, Director of *Alien*, Creates Another Science Fiction Masterwork, *Blade Runner*', publicity release, p. 2.

6 Paul Sammon, *Future Noir: The Making of* Blade Runner (New York: HarperCollins, 1996), p. 73.

7 This is brilliantly discussed by Annette Michelson in 'Bodies in Space: Film as "Carnal Knowledge"', *Artforum* vol. 7 no. 6 (1969), pp. 54–63.

8 Oliver Sacks, 'To See and Not See', in *An Anthropologist on Mars: Seven Paradoxical Tales* (New York: Alfred A. Knopf, 1995), p. 114.

9 Ibid., p. 136 (his emphasis, followed by my emphasis).

10 Georg Simmel, 'The Metropolis and Mental Life', in Donald N. Levine (ed.), *On Individuality and Social Forms* (Chicago: University of Chicago Press, 1971), p. 325.

11 Ibid., pp. 334–5.

12 Ibid., pp. 330, 334.

13 Ibid., p. 328.

14 Sammon, *Future Noir*, p. 59.

15 These figures are from Sammon, *Future Noir*; Kenneth Turan reported in the *Los Angeles Times Magazine* (13 September 1992) that each partner put in $8.5 million.

16 See Leo Marx, *The Machine in the Garden: Technology and the Pastoral Ideal in America* (New York: Oxford University Press, 1964), chapter 5.

17 *Blade Runner* production notes, p. 5.

18 Syd Mead, *OBLAGON: Concepts of Syd Mead* (Japanese publication, imported by Oblagon Inc., Los Angeles, 1985), p. 12.

19 Herb A. Lightman and Richard Patterson, '*Blade Runner*: Production Design and Photography', *American Cinematographer* vol. 63 no. 7 (1982), pp. 717–18; Sammon, *Future Noir*, p. 77.

20 Sammon, *Future Noir*, p. 79.

21 This is discussed by Yuricich's assistant, Rocco Gioffre, in Sammon, *Future Noir*, p. 257.

22 This remark is made in an interview with Don Shay presented on the Criterion laser disk of *Close Encounters of the Third Kind*.

23 For more on Trumbull's effects, see my 'The Artificial Infinite: On Special Effects and the Sublime', in Lynne Cook and Peter Wollen (eds), *Visual Display: Culture beyond Appearances* (Seattle: Bay Press, 1995), pp. 254–89.

24 See Sammon, *Future Noir*, pp. 226, 264–5.

25 Ibid., pp. 230, 235.

26 'The Futuristic Cars of *Blade Runner*', publicity release, p. 1; Mead, *OBLAGON*, p. 102; Herb A. Lightman, '*Blade Runner*: Special Photographic Effects', *American Cinematographer* vol. 63 no. 7 (1982), p. 726.

27 As on *Citizen Kane*, all the sets on *Blade Runner* had ceilings.

28 Lightman and Patterson, 'Production Design'.

29 Ibid., p. 723.

30 Paul Sammon cites an associate of Scott's on this point in *Future Noir*, p. 206.

31 Pauline Kael, 'Baby, the Rain Must Fall', *The New Yorker*, 12 July 1982, p. 85.
32 Janet Maslin, *New York Times*, 25 June 1982; Gene Siskel, *Chicago Tribune*, 25 June 1982.
33 Sammon, *Future Noir*, pp. 316, 318.
34 Ibid., p. 322.
35 Sobchack's *Screening Space*, 2nd edn (New York: Ungar Press, 1987) provides a particularly useful mapping of *Blade Runner*'s post-modern attributes.
36 Sammon, *Future Noir*, p. 368.
37 While some of the film's visual designs are evidently stolen from *Horizons*, the utopian manifesto by industrial designer Norman Bel Geddes, the city of the future actually anticipates his Futurama pavilion at the 1939 New York World's Fair.
38 Raoul Vaneigem, 'Basic Banalities', trans. by Ken Knabb, in Knabb (ed.), *Situationist International Anthology* (Berkeley, CA: Bureau of Public Secrets, 1981), p. 128.
39 J.G. Ballard, 'The Concentration City', in *The Best Short Stories of J.G. Ballard* (New York: Holt, Rinehart and Winston, 1978), pp. 1–20.
40 Moebius has extensive connections to science fiction cinema: he has collaborated with film-makers Dan O'Bannon, scriptwriter of *Dark Star* (1974) and *Alien*

(1979), and Alexander Jodorowsky. In addition, Moebius contributed costume designs to *Alien*, *Tron* (1982) and *The Abyss* (1990).
41 Fredric Jameson, 'Progress vs. Utopia; or, Can We Imagine the Future?', *Science Fiction Studies* vol. 9 no. 2 (1982), p. 152.
42 See my *Terminal Identity: The Virtual Subject in Postmodern Science Fiction* (Durham, NC: Duke University, 1993).
43 William Sharpe and Leonard Wallock, 'From "Great Town" to "Nonplace Urban Realm": Reading the Modern City', in Sharpe and Wallock (eds), *Visions of the Modern City: Essays in History, Art and Literature* (Baltimore: The Johns Hopkins University Press, 1987), p. 11.
44 See Melvin M. Webber, 'The Urban Place and the Nonplace Urban Realm', in Webber et al. (eds), *Explorations into Urban Structure* (Philadelphia: University of Pennsylvania Press, 1964), pp. 79–153.
45 Maurice Merleau-Ponty, *Phenomenology of Perception*, trans. by Colin Smith (London: Routledge & Kegan Paul, 1962), p. 142.
46 See Vermeer's *A Lady at the Virginal with a Gentleman* (*The Music Lesson*) (1662–4) and Jan van Eyck's *Madonna with Canon van der Paele* (1436). Relevant Hopper

paintings would include *Eleven AM* (1926), *Hotel Room* (1931), *Room in New York* (1932) and *Office at Night* (1940).
47 Jameson, *Postmodernism*, p. 419n.
48 Bruce Sterling, 'Preface', in Bruce Sterling (ed.), *Mirrorshades: The Cyberpunk Anthology* (New York: Arbor House, 1986), p. xi.
49 The phrase is Syd Mead's (Lightman and Patterson, 'Production Design', p. 687), the comparisons are mine.
50 Fredric Jameson, 'On Chandler', in Glenn W. Most and William W. Stowe (eds), *The Poetics of Murder: Detective Fiction and Literary Theory* (New York: Harcourt Brace Jovanovich, 1983), p. 131.
51 Rem Koolhaas, *Delirious New York* (New York: Monacelli Press, 1994), p. 123.
52 Ann Douglas, *Terrible Honesty: Mongrel Manhattan in the 1920s* (New York: Farrar, Straus and Giroux, 1995), p. 452.
53 Ibid., p. 453.
54 Koolhaas, *Delirious New York*, p. 33.
55 Ibid., p. 62.
56 Wolfgang Schivelbusch, *The Railway Journey: The Industrialization of Time and Space in the 19th Century* (Berkeley: University of California Press, 1986), p. 191.
57 Sammon, *Future Noir*, p. 249.

58 *Sunrise* was written by Carl Mayer, photographed by Karl Struss and Charles Rosher and directed by F.W. Murnau, all of whom deserve mention.

59 Leo Charney, 'In a Moment: Film and the Philosophy of Modernity', in Leo Charney and Vanessa R. Schwartz (eds), *Cinema and the Invention of Modern Life* (Berkeley: University of California Press, 1996), p. 292.

60 Ibid.

61 James Gleick, *Chaos: Making a New Science* (New York: Viking Books, 1987), p. 98.

62 Douglas, *Terrible Honesty*, p. 448.

63 Cited in Dietrich Neumann, 'Before and After *Metropolis*: Film and Architecture in Search of the Modern City', in Dietrich Neumann (ed.), *Film Architecture: From* Metropolis *to* Blade Runner (New York: Prestel-Verlag, 1996), p. 34.

64 See J.P. Telotte, *Replications: A Robotic History of the Science Fiction Film* (Urbana: University of Illinois Press, 1996), chapter 2.

65 Sammon, *Future Noir*, p. 75.

66 Ibid., p. 97.

67 Steve Carper, 'Subverting the Disaffected City: Cityscape in *Blade Runner*', in Judith B. Kernan (ed.), *Retrofitting Blade Runner* (Bowling Green, OH: Bowling Green State University Popular Press, 1991), p. 186.

68 Sammon, *Future Noir*, p. 111.

69 Michael Webb, '"Like Today, Only More So": The Credible Dystopia of *Blade Runner*', in Neumann (ed.), *Film Architecture*, p. 44.

70 Sterling, 'Preface', p. xi.

71 Guy Debord, *Society of the Spectacle* (Detroit: Black & Red, 1983), §29 [n.p.].

72 Ibid., §30.

73 From a 1976 author's note to 'Colony', reprinted in *The Collected Stories of Philip K. Dick*, vol. 1 (New York: Carol Publishing, 1987), p. 404.

74 Cited in Sammon, *Future Noir*, p. 16.

75 Ibid., p. 285.

76 Norman Spinrad, 'The Transmogrification of Philip K. Dick', in *Science Fiction in the Real World* (Carbondale, IL: Southern Illinois University Press, 1990), p. 210.

77 Simmel, 'The Metropolis and Mental Life', p. 326.

78 Ibid., p. 330.

79 Schivelbusch, *Railway Journey*, p. 143.

80 Donna Haraway, 'A Cyborg Manifesto: Science, Technology and Socialist-Feminism in the 1980s', in *Simians, Cyborgs, and Women* (New York: Routledge, 1989), p. 152.

81 Ibid., p. 180.

82 Michel Foucault, *The Order of Things* (New York: Vintage Books, 1973), p. xxiii.

83 Haraway, 'Cyborg Manifesto', p. 150.

84 Sammon, *Future Noir*, p. 376.

85 Roland Barthes, *Camera Lucida*, trans. by Richard Howard (New York: Hill and Wang, 1981), p. 81. Cited in Kaja Silverman, 'Back to the Future', *Camera Obscura* no. 27 (1991), p. 14. Silverman notes that it is has become a commonplace to refer to Barthes in discussions of *Blade Runner*.

86 Cited in Oliver Sacks, 'The Landscape of His Dreams', in *Anthropologist on Mars*, p. 175.

87 Oliver Sacks, 'The Lost Mariner', in *The Man Who Mistook His Wife for a Hat* (New York: Alfred A. Knopf, 1985), p. 41. Luis Buñuel, *My Last Sigh* (New York: Vintage Books, 1984), pp. 4–5. Sammon, *Future Noir*, p. 364.

88 Knopf, 1985), p. 41. Luis Buñuel, *My Last Sigh* (New York: Vintage Books, 1984), pp. 4–5. Sammon, *Future Noir*, p. 364.

89 This clever clue was spotted by Dietrich Neumann, an architectural historian, in *Film Architecture*, p. 152.

90 Noël Carroll, 'Interpreting *Citizen Kane*', *Persistence of Vision* no. 7 (1989).

91 Sammon, *Future Noir*, p. 133.

92 Ibid., p. 364.

93 Slavoj Žižek, 'I or He or It (the Thing) Which Thinks', in *Tarrying with the Negative: Kant, Hegel, and the Critique of Ideology* (Durham, NC: Duke University Press, 1993), pp. 9–44.

94 Žižek makes an identical point about virtual reality:

'true the computer-generated "virtual reality" is a semblance, it does foreclose the Real; but what we experience as the "true, hard, external reality" is based upon exactly the same exclusion. The ultimate lesson of "virtual reality" is the virtualization of the very "true" reality: by the mirage of "virtual reality," the "true" reality itself is posited as a semblance of itself, as a pure symbolic edifice.' Ibid., p. 44.

95 Ibid., p. 41.

96 Ibid., p. 15.

97 Sammon, *Future Noir*, p. 178.

98 Koolhaas, *Delirious New York*, p. 130.

99 See the draft dated 24 July 1980, p. 100. Reprinted by Script City in Hollywood, CA.

100 Richard Dyer, 'Judy Garland and Gay Men', in *Heavenly Bodies: Film Stars and Society* (London: Macmillan, 1986), pp. 141–94.

101 Like Holly Golightly in *Breakfast at Tiffany's*, Roy Batty is 'a phony', but he's 'a *real* phony'.

102 Žižek, 'I or He or It', p. 41.

103 Simmel, 'Metropolis and Mental Life', p. 339.

Credits

BLADE RUNNER
USA, 1982, 117 min.
Directors Cut, 1992, 112 min.
Production company
Blade Runner Partnership.
A Michael Deeley-Ridley
Scott production. A Jerry
Perechino and Bud Yorkin
presentation. A Tandem
Productions presentation.
A Ladd Company Release
in association with
Sir Run Run Shaw through
Warner Bros.
Executive producers
Brian Kelly, Hampton
Fancher
Producer
Michael Deeley
Associate producer
Ivor Powell
**Executive in charge of
production**
C.O. Erickson
Production executive
Katherine Haber
Unit production manager
John W. Rogers
Location manager
Michael Neale
Production co-ordinator
Vickie Alper
Production controller
Steve Warner
Auditor
Dick Dubuque
Assistant auditor
Kelly Marshall
Producer's assistant
Bryan Haynes
**Assistant location
manager**
Greg Hamlin

Payroll
Paulette Fina
Director
Ridley Scott
First assistant directors
Newton Arnold, Peter
Cornberg
Second assistant directors
Don Hauer, Morris Chapnick,
Richard Schroer
DGA trainee
Victoria Rhodes
Script supervisor
Anna Maria Quintana
Casting
Mike Fenton, Jane Feinberg
Additional casting
Marci Liroff
Screenplay
Hampton Fancher, David
Peoples. Based on the novel
*Do Androids Dream of
Electric Sheep?* by Philip K.
Dick
Director of photography
Jordan Cronenweth
Additional photography
Steven Poster, Brian Tufano
Camera operators
Robert Thomas, Albert
Bettcher, Dick Colean
First assistant camera
Mike Genne, Steve Smith
Second assistant camera
George D. Greer
Lighting gaffer
Dick Hart
Best boy
Joseph W. Cardoza Jr
Key grip
Carey Griffith
Best boy grip
Robert E. Winger

Dolly grip
Donald A. Schmitz
Crab dolly grip
Douglas G. Willas
Supervising editor
Terry Rawlings
Editor
Marsha Nakashima
Assistant editor
William Zabala
**First assistant editor
(English editing)**
Les Healey
Production designer
Lawrence G. Paull
Art director
David Snyder
Visual futurist
Syd Mead
Set decorators
Linda DeScenna,
Tom Roysden,
Leslie Frankenheimer
Production illustrators
Sherman Labby, Mentor
Huebner, Tom Southwell
Assistant art director
Stephen Dane
Set designers
Tom Duffield, Bill Skinner,
Greg Pickrell, Charles Breen,
Louis Mann, David Klasson
Leadman
Michael Taylor
Construction co-ordinator
James F. Orendorf
**Assistant construction co-
ordinator**
Alfred J. Litteken
Construction clerk
James Hale
Painting co-ordinator
James T. Woods

Stand-by painter
Buzz Lombardo
Property master
Terry Lewis
Assistant property
David Quick, Arthur Shippee
Jr, John A. Scott III
Costume designers
Charles Knode, Michael
Kaplan
Men's costumers
James Lapidus,
Bobby E. Horn
Ladies' costumers
Winnie Brown,
Linda A. Matthews
Make-up artist
Marvin G. Westmore
Hairstylist
Shirley L. Padgett
**Special photography
effects**
Entertainment Effects Group
**Special photography
effects supervisors**
Douglas Trumbull,
Richard Yuricich,
David Dryer
**Special photography
effects director of
photography**
Dave Stewart
**Optical photography
supervisor**
Robert Hall
**Optical photography
cameramen**
Don Baker, Rupert Benson,
Glen Campbell, Charles
Cowles, David Hardberger,
Ronald Longo, Timothy
McHugh, John Seay
Matte artist
Matthew Yuricich
Additional matte artist
Michele Moen

Matte photography
Robert Bailey, Tama
Takahashi, Don Jarel
Special camera technician
Alan Harding
Optical line-up
Philip Barberio,
Richard Ripple
Animation/graphics
John Wash
Effects illustrator
Tom Cranham
**Special projects
consultant**
Wayne Smith
Miniature technician
Bob Spurlock
Assistant effects editor
Michael Bakauskas
Chief model maker
Mark Stetson
Model makers
Jerry Allen, Sean Casey,
Paul Curley, Leslie Ekker,
Thomas Field, Vance
Frederick, William George,
Kristopher Gregg,
Robert Johnston, Michael
McMillian, Thomas Phak,
Christopher Ross,
Robert Wilcox
Key grip
Pat Van Auken
Gaffer
Gary Randall
Film co-ordinator
Jack Hinkle
Cinetechnician
George Polkinghorne
Still lab
Virgil Mirano
**Electronic and mechanical
design**
Evans Westmore
Electronic engineering
Greg McMurry

Computer engineering
Richard Hollander
**Special engineering
consultants**
Bud Elam, David Crafton
Production office manager
Joyce Goldberg
Visual effects auditor
Dina Gold
Assistant to David Dryer
Leora Glass
Visual displays
Dream Quest Inc.
**Electron microscope
photographs**
David Scharf
Esper sequences
Filmfex, Lodge/Cheesman
**Special floor effects
supervisor**
Terry Frazee
**Special effects
technicians**
Steve Galich, Logan Frazee,
William G. Curtis
Transportation captain
Howard Davidson
Transportation co-captain
James Sharp
Craft service
Michael Knutsen
Publicist
Saul Kahan
Stills
Stephen Vaughan
Titles
Intralink Film Graphic Design
**Music/music
arranger/music
performer/music producer**
Vangelis
Production mixer
Bud Alper
**Sound editor (English
editing)**
Peter Pennell

**Assistant sound editor
(English editing)**
Peter Gallagher
**Dialogue Editor (English
editing)**
Michael Hopkins
**Assistant dialogue editor
(English editing)**
Peter Baldock
Chief dubbing mixers
Graham V. Hartstone
(Pinewood Studios),
Gerry Humphries
(Twickenham Studios)
Boom man
Eugene Byron Ashbrook
Cableman
Beau Baker
Stunt co-ordinator
Gary Combs
Stuntpersons
Ray Bickel, Janet Brady,
Diane Carter, Ann Chatterton,
Gilbert Combs, Anthony Cox,
Rita Egleston, Gerry Epper,
Jeannie Epper, James Halty,
Jeffrey Imada, Gary McLarty,
Karen McLarty, Beth Nufer,
Roy Ogata, Bobby Porter,
Lee Pulford, Ruth Redfern,
George Sawaya, Charles
Tamburro, Jack Tyree, Mike
Washlake, Michael Zurich
Action prop supervisor
Mike Fink
Action prop consultant
Linda Fleisher

Harrison Ford
Rick Deckard
Rutger Hauer
Roy Batty
Sean Young
Rachael
Edward James Olmos
Gaff
M. Emmet Walsh
Captain Bryant
Daryl Hannah
Pris
William Sanderson
J.F. Sebastian
Brion James
Leon
Joe Turkel
Doctor Tyrell
Joanna Cassidy
Zhora
James Hong
Chew
Morgan Paull
Holden
Kevin Thompson
Bear
John Edward Allen
Kaiser
Hy Pyke
Taffey Lewis
Kimiro Hiroshige
Cambodian lady
Robert Okazaki
Sushi master
Carolyn DeMirjian
Saleslady
**Charles Knapp, Leo
Gorcey Jr, Thomas
Hutchinson**
Bartenders
Kelly Hine
Show girl
**Sharon Hesky, Rose
Mascari**
Barflies

**Susan Rhee, Hiroko
Kimuri**
Geishas
Kai Wong, Kit Wong
Chinese men
**Hiro Okazaki, Steve Pope,
Robert Reiter**
Policemen

Bibliography

I am obviously indebted to Paul Sammon's *Future Noir: The Making of* Blade Runner (New York: HarperCollins, 1996) for information on the film's production and reception. I recommend to readers who would like more detail about *all* aspects of the film, its various versions and its audience.

Ballard, J.G., 'The Concentration City', in *The Best Short Stories of J.G. Ballard* (New York: Holt, Rinehart and Winston, 1978), pp. 1–20.

Barthes, Roland, *Camera Lucida*, trans. by Richard Howard (New York: Hill and Wang, 1981).

Baudrillard, Jean, *Simulations. Foreign Agents Series*, trans. by Paul Foss, Paul Patton and Philip Beitchman (New York: Semiotext(e), 1983).

Bellamy, Edward, *Looking Backward* (New York: Penguin, 1982). Originally published in 1888.

Bruno, Guiliana, 'Ramble City: Postmodernism and *Blade Runner*', *October* no. 41 (1987), pp. 61–74.

Bukatman, Scott, '*Terminal Identity: The Virtual Subject in Postmodern Science Fiction* (Durham, NC: Duke University Press, 1993).

—, 'The Artificial Intimate: On Special Effects and the Sublime', in Lynne Cook and Peter Wollen (eds), *Visual Display: Culture beyond Appearances* (Bay Press, 1995), pp. 254–89.

Buñuel, Luis, *My Last Sigh*, trans. by Abigail Israel (New York: Vintage Books, 1984).

Carper, Steve, 'Subverting the Disaffected City: Cityscape in *Blade Runner*', in Judith B. Kernan (ed.), *Retrofitting* Blade Runner (Bowling Green, OH: Bowling Green State University Popular Press, 1991), pp. 185–95.

Carroll, Noël, 'Interpreting Citizen Kane', *Persistence of Vision* no. 7 (1989), pp. 51–62.

Charney, Leo, 'In a Moment: Film and the Philosophy of Modernity', in Charney and Vanessa R. Schwartz (eds), *Cinema and the Invention of Modern Life* (Berkeley: University of California Press, 1996), pp. 279–94.

Cinemania 96. Computer software. Microsoft Corporation, 1996.

Debord, Guy, *Society of the Spectacle* (Detroit: Black & Red, 1983). Originally published in 1967; originally translated in 1970, revised in 1977.

Delany, Samuel R., 'About 5,750 Words', in *The Jewel-Hinged Jaw: Notes on the Language of Science Fiction* (Elizabethtown, NY: Dragon Press, 1977), pp. 33–49.

—, *Starboard Wine: More Notes on the Language of Science Fiction* (Elizabethtown, NY: Dragon Press, 1984).

Dick, Philip K., *Do Androids Dream of Electric Sheep?* (New York: Ballantine Books, 1968).

—, *UBIK: The Screenplay* (Minneapolis: Corroboree Press, 1985).

—, 'Colony', reprinted in *The Collected Stories of Philip K. Dick*, vol. 1 (New York: Carol Publishing, 1987), p. 404.

Douglas, Ann, *Terrible Honesty: Mongrel Manhattan in the 1920s* (New York: Farrar, Straus and Giroux, 1995).

Dyer, Richard, 'Judy Garland and Gay Men', in *Heavenly Bodies: Film Stars and Society* (London: Macmillan, 1986), pp. 141–94.

Finch, Christopher, *Special Effects: Creating Movie Magic* (New York: Abbeville Press, 1984).

Foucault, Michel, *The Order of Things: An Archeology of the Human Sciences* (New York: Vintage Books, 1973).

Gibson, William, *Neuromancer* (New York: Ace Books, 1984).

Gleick, James, *Chaos: Making a New Science* (New York: Viking Books, 1987).

Grolier Science Fiction: The Multimedia Encyclopedia

of Science Fiction. Computer software. Grolier Electronic Publishing, 1995.

Haraway, Donna, 'A Cyborg Manifesto: Science, Technology and Socialist-Feminism in the 1980s', in *Simians, Cyborgs, and Women* (New York: Routledge, 1989), pp. 149–81.

Heath, Stephen, 'Narrative Space', in *Questions of Cinema* (Bloomington: Indiana University Press, 1981), pp. 19–75.

Jameson, Fredric, 'Progress vs. Utopia; or, Can We Imagine the Future?', *Science Fiction Studies* vol. 9 no. 2 (1982), pp. 147–58.

—, 'On Chandler', in Glenn W. Most and William W. Stowe (eds), *The Poetics of Murder: Detective Fiction and Literary Theory* (New York: Harcourt Brace Jovanovich, 1983), pp. 122–48.

—, *Postmodernism, or the Cultural Logic of Late Capitalism* (Durham, NC: Duke University Press, 1991).

—, 'Science Fiction as a Spatial Genre: Generic Discontinuities and the Problem of Figuration in Vonda McIntyre's *The Exile Waiting*', *Science Fiction Studies* vol. 14 no. 1 (1987), pp. 44–59.

Kael, Pauline, 'Baby, the Rain Must Fall', *The New Yorker*, 12 July 1982, pp. 82–5.

Kernan, Judith B. (ed.), *Retrofitting Blade Runner* (Bowling Green, OH: Bowling Green State University

Popular Press, 1991).

Koolhaas, Rem, *Delirious New York* (New York: Monacelli Press, 1994). Originally published in 1978.

Landon, Brooks, *The Aesthetics of Ambivalence: Rethinking Science Fiction in the Age of Electronic (Re)Production* (Westport, CT: Greenwood Press, 1992).

Lightman, Herb A., '*Blade Runner*: Special Photographic Effects', *American Cinematographer* vol. 63 no. 7 (1982), pp. 692–3, 725–32. Interview with David Dryer.

Lightman, Herb A. and Richard Patterson, '*Blade Runner*: Production Design and Photography', *American Cinematographer* vol. 63 no. 7 (1982), pp. 684–91, 715–25.

Marx, Leo, *The Machine in the Garden: Technology and the Pastoral Ideal in America* (New York: Oxford University Press, 1964).

Mead, Syd, 'Designing the Future', in Danny Peary (ed.), *Omni's Screen Flights, Screen Fantasies* (Garden City, NY: Doubleday & Co, 1984), pp. 199–213.

—, *OBLAGON: Concepts of Syd Mead* (Japanese publication, imported by Oblagon Inc., Los Angeles, 1985).

Merleau-Ponty, Maurice, *Phenomenology of Perception*, trans. by Colin Smith (London: Routledge & Kegan Paul, 1962).

Michelson, Annette, 'Bodies in Space: Film as "Carnal Knowledge"', *Artforum* vol. 7 no. 6 (1969), pp. 54–63.

Neumann, Dietrich, 'Before and After *Metropolis*: Film and Architecture in Search of the Modern City', in Neumann (ed.), *Film Architecture: From* Metropolis *to* Blade Runner (New York: Prestel-Verlag, 1996), pp. 33–8.

Ross, Andrew, 'Cyberpunk in Boystown', in *Strange Weather: Culture, Science and Technology in an Age of Limits* (London: Verso, 1991), pp. 137–67.

Sacks, Oliver, 'The Lost Mariner', in *The Man Who Mistook His Wife for a Hat* (New York: Alfred A. Knopf, 1985), pp. 22–41.

—, 'The Landscape of His Dreams', in *An Anthropologist on Mars: Seven Paradoxical Tales* (New York: Alfred A. Knopf, 1995), pp. 153–87.

—, 'To See and Not See', in *An Anthropologist on Mars: Seven Paradoxical Tales* (New York: Alfred A. Knopf, 1995), pp. 108–52.

Schivelbusch, Wolfgang, *The Railway Journey: The Industrialization of Time and Space in the 19th Century* (Berkeley: University of California Press, 1986). Originally published in German in 1977.

Sharpe, William and Leonard Wallock, 'From "Great Town" to "Nonplace

Urban Realm": Reading the Modern City', in Sharpe and Wallock (eds), *Visions of the Modern City: Essays in History, Art and Literature* (Baltimore: Johns Hopkins University Press, 1987), pp. 1–50.

Silverman, Kaja, 'Back to the Future', *Camera Obscura* no. 27 (1991), pp. 109–32.

Simmel, Georg, 'The Metropolis and Mental Life', in Donald N. Levine (ed.), *On Individuality and Social Forms* (Chicago: University of Chicago Press, 1971), pp. 324–39. Originally published in 1903.

Sobchack, Vivian, *Screening Space: The American Science Fiction Film*, 2nd edn (New York: Ungar Press, 1987).

Spinrad, Norman, 'The Transmogrification of Philip K. Dick', in *Science Fiction in the Real World* (Carbondale, IL: Southern Illinois University Press, 1990), pp. 198–216.

Sterling, Bruce, 'Preface', in Bruce Sterling (ed.), *Mirrorshades: The Cyberpunk Anthology* (New York: Arbor House, 1986), pp. vii–xiv.

Telotte, J.P., *Replications: A Robotic History of the Science Fiction Film* (Urbana: University of Illinois Press, 1996).

Turan, Kenneth, '*Blade Runner* 2', *Los Angeles Times Magazine*, 13 September 1992, pp. 19–24.

Vaneigem, Raoul, 'Basic Banalities', trans. by Ken Knabb, in Knabb (ed.), *Situationist International Anthology* (Berkeley, CA: Bureau of Public Secrets, 1981), pp. 118–33.

Webb, Michael, '"Like Today, Only More So": The Credible Dystopia of *Blade Runner*,' in Dietrich Neumann (ed.), *Film Architecture: From* Metropolis *to* Blade Runner (New York: Prestel-Verlag, 1996), pp. 44–7.

Webber, Melvin M., 'The Urban Place and the Nonplace Urban Realm,' in Webber et al. (eds), *Explorations into Urban Structure* (Philadelphia: University of Pennsylvania Press, 1964), pp. 79–153.

Žižek, Slavoj, 'I or He or It (the Thing) Which Thinks', in *Tarrying with the Negative: Kant, Hegel, and the Critique of Ideology* (Durham, NC: Duke University Press, 1993), pp. 9–44.

Web Sites

2019: Off World [http://kzsu.stanford.edu/uwi/br/off-world.html]

The Blade Runner FAQ [http://www.uq.oz.au/~csmchapm/bladerunner/]

BFI Modern Classics is an exciting new series which combines careful research with high quality writing about contemporary cinema. Authors write on a film of their choice, making the case for its elevation to the status of classic. The series will grow into an influential and authoritative commentary on all that is best in the cinema of our time.
If you would like to receive further information about future **BFI Modern Classics** or about other books on film, media and popular culture from BFI Publishing, please fill in your name and address and return this card to the BFI*.
No stamp needed if posted in the UK, Channel Islands, or Isle of Man.

NAME

ADDRESS

POSTCODE

* North America: Please return your card to:
Indiana University Press, Attn: LPB, 601 N Morton Street,
Bloomington, IN 47401-3797